Don't Waste Your Wastes — Compost 'em

The Homeowner's Guide To Recycling Yard Wastes

by Bert Whitehead

❖

SUNNYVALE PRESS
P.O. Box 851971
Mesquite, Texas 75185–1971

Library of Congress Cataloging Number: 91-66324

ISBN 0-9630612-0-8

Printed and Distributed by Taylor Publishing Company, Dallas, Texas

Dedicated to my children,

my grandchildren,

and all future generations.

ACKNOWLEDGEMENTS

I wish to give a special "thanks" to the following people who so willingly gave their time and assistance: Clarence G. Golueke, Ph.D., professor emeritus, University of California at Berkeley, for being so patient and helpful to an unknown caller inquiring about his "14 Day Method" research; Richard M. Kashmanian, Ph.D., Regulatory Innovations Staff, U.S. Environmental Protection Agency, Washington, D.C., for his quick response to my requests for EPA documents; R. Garland Ross, City Secretary, Quitman, Texas, for opening my eyes to the seriousness of the landfill situation in rural communities; Bob Moseley, Manager, Solid Waste Disposal District, City of Dallas, and Carlos Rovelo, Recycling Coordinator, City of Dallas, for their updated landfill and recycling information, respectively; Samuel D. Cotner, Ph.D., Associate Department Head and Extension Program Leader, The Texas A&M University System, for his review and technical advice; Stacy Reese, County Agent-Horticulture, Texas Agricultural Extension Service, Dallas, Texas, for continually helping to increase my knowledge of horticulture; Linda Muhl and Debby Rottman, for their superb proofing, editing, and typing of my manuscript; Warren G. Frazier, for his photographic advice and assistance; I. J. (Jack) Russum, who has been my best friend for over forty-five years, for his counseling and guidance; The Color Lab, Inc., Dallas, for their excellent photographic service; Jay Love and all of the good people at Taylor Publishing Company for their help in printing this book; and Lucy, my wife for thirty-eight years, for her love and encouragement.

Photography

All of the photographs included in this book were taken by the author. The photograph of the author and his grandchildren on the front cover was taken by Warren G. Frazier.

Bert Whitehead

ABOUT THE AUTHOR

In 1986 Bert took an early retirement from Southwestern Bell Telephone Company in Dallas, Texas. The following year he enrolled in the Texas Agricultural Extension Service's Master Gardener Training Program, and he has been doing volunteer work as a Texas Master Gardener since that time. He has made numerous talks on "How To Make Compost" at garden clubs and convention centers in the Dallas/Fort Worth metroplex, using colored slides of some of the composting methods which he has refined since he first began making compost in 1980. During the past year, some of his composting techniques have also been featured in *The Dallas Morning News,* the *Dallas Times Herald,* and in the *Fort Worth Star-Telegram.* This is his first book and *the* first book to be published which illustrates and describes in detail these various methods of composting.

A native of New Orleans, Louisiana, Bert moved to Dallas in 1945 and began his career with the telephone company. He continues to be involved in volunteer work with the Telephone Pioneers of America, in fund-raising activities for the Scottish Rite's Hospital For Crippled Children, and (along with his wife) in assisting the Visiting Nurses Association's "Meals on Wheels" program. He and his wife, the former Lucille Lee of Quitman, Texas, also enjoy spending time with their two children and three grandchildren.

Jay Love
Consultant for Publications
Taylor Publishing Company

❖

Contents

❖

Introduction

Those of us who care about our country and the environment in which we live, and the one which we will be passing on to our children and grandchildren, must be aware of the need to greatly reduce the millions of tons of wastes which we are presently sending to our landfill sites each year. We must stop wasting our wastes!

The United States Environmental Protection Agency's study, Yard Waste Composting — A Study of Eight Programs (EPA Document #530-SW-89-038) which was completed in April 1989, states that almost "one-third of the Municipal Solid Waste (MSW) landfills in this country are expected to reach capacity between 5 and 7 years from now (Porter, 1988) while new landfills are difficult to site." The 160 million tons of garbage we are presently generating annually is expected to reach almost 200 million tons by the year 2000. The study estimated that yard wastes such as grass clippings, leaves, tree and shrub prunings account for almost twenty percent of this garbage each year. And, during the summer and fall months yard wastes can represent up to *fifty percent* of the total MSW stream.

The main thrust and purpose of the EPA study was to look at the "methods and products of yard waste composting in the context of 8 programs currently in operation in the U.S., in order to provide information and options to communities faced with difficult choices in the area of MSW management."

Unlike the EPA study, this book will focus on providing you, personally, with a sensible guide, using simple methods which will enable you to benefit from the recycling and composting of your own yard and kitchen wastes.

You and I can not only have a positive effect on reducing the large amounts of wastes being sent to our rapidly filling landfills, but we can also benefit by greatly improving the soils in our lawns, shrub and flower beds, and vegetable gardens. And, we will be saving money by purchasing fewer plastic trash bags, using less water, and less fertilizer. (Chapter 1 will explain the many uses of compost which make some of these savings possible.)

The methods of making compost which are explained in great detail in this book are those which I have found to be successful during the ten years I have been making compost. Even if you have never made compost before you will find, as I have, that making compost is not complicated. In fact, you will be amazed at how easy it is to make compost!

I believe you will find this text's "tell me, show me" instructional approach which is listed below most helpful:

1. You will be given the correct quantities and types of ingredients to use, literally recipes to follow, for each of the methods described and illustrated.

2. The color photographs of the different types of enclosures and containers, along with an explanation of how they can be made (if you choose to make your own) and how to use them, should help you decide which method is best for you.

3. The sequence of colored pictures taken each time a compost pile is turned during the "Fastest Method" of composting, from start to finish, will show you exactly what to expect when using this method.

4. The compost temperature chart will graphically depict the desired build up of heat when using this same method, along with the effect which turning the pile has on maximizing this heat build up.

You and I, individually, can use our grass clippings, leaves, and kitchen wastes and make better compost than that which can be made by any municipal composting facility. Whether young or old, rich or poor, strong or weak, you can make compost by using any of the methods described in Chapters 4 through 8.

If making your own compost does not appeal to you for some reason, you will still find herein a number of easy ways to make use of your yard and kitchen wastes and reap most of the benefits previously mentioned.

Although this book was written primarily to show what we home owners can do to help slow down the fast approaching landfill crisis and to benefit the people who live in city and suburban areas, those who live in the country or on farms and ranches can also benefit by using these methods. The adverse effects of this crisis are not limited to people in metropolitan areas. Those who live in rural areas are being affected just as much, if not more so. This is truly a *national* problem which we citizens can help solve *literally* "in our own back yards" by recycling our kitchen and yard wastes.

Let me give a couple of examples of the seriousness of the landfill problem, one in a rural area, and one in a metropolitan area.

On October 27, 1990, I met with Mr. Garland Ross, the City Secretary of Quitman, Texas. Quitman has a population of about nineteen hundred people (about 900 households) and is located approximately eighty-five miles east of Dallas in Wood county. I accompanied Mr. Ross to Quitman's 5-acre landfill site, which has been in use by that community since 1948.

Mr. Ross explained that beginning in 1948, all wastes were put into a trench and set on fire at this site. As more wastes were collected, they were put into the same trench and burned, and this procedure was continued until the trench was filled with ashes. Soil dug from an adjacent trench was then used to cover the ashes and to fill the previous trench, and so on. By the end of the 1970s, the flies, odor and smoke settlement worsened to the extent that the city voted a bond to finance the purchase of an incinerator and the construction of the building required for the incinerator.

Beginning in 1981, the incinerator was used to burn house-hold and yard wastes. The incinerator's ashes were spread on top of the previously used trenches with a light covering of soil placed on top of the ashes. This procedure was continued until (as a result of passage of the Clean Air Act) they were told to stop burning yard wastes in the incinerator. Since September 1, 1990, only household garbage can be incinerated, and all yard wastes are put into piles to be decomposed by Mother Nature at the landfill site.

Currently, each household in Quitman is paying $17.84 per

month for waste collection and disposal. This amount is forecasted to be needed each month for the next year to cover the anticipated costs associated with the closing of the landfill and the installation of monitoring devices for the incinerator's smokestack, as well as for the collection of wastes. Upon completion of the landfill closure and the installation of the monitoring devices, the individual household waste collection cost is expected to be around $10.00 per month.

Concurrently, Wood county and several adjoining counties, including Camp, Rains, Upshur, and that part of Smith county north of Interstate 20, are to locate a mutually agreed upon landfill site and form a Solid Waste Disposal District to service their combined populations. *(See Picture #1 below, and Pictures #2 and #3 on Pages 13 and 14.)*

The City of Dallas's landfill site is situated on 2,039 acres of

Picture #1

This approximately 1-1/2 acres of Quitman's 5-acre landfill site is in the process of being closed. The mound of sandy clay soil at the left edge was the first load deposited to begin forming a sloping mound on top of the area to conform to runoff specifications.

land that was purchased in 1974, at a cost of $1,000.00 per acre. Only 965 acres are permitted for actual landfilling, however, with the remaining acreage providing a greenbelt buffer zone between this operation and the surrounding neighborhoods.

Landfilling operations began in 1980, and this site has received nearly one million tons of wastes each year since that time, filling about 200 acres to date. An average of 900 vehicles unload a *daily* average of about 3,700 *tons* of municipal and commercial wastes. No liquids, Class 1 industrial wastes, or hazardous wastes are accepted.

Dallas residents are presently paying $7.00 per month for waste collection and disposal.

Picture #2
This shows two mounds of yard wastes at the Quitman, Texas, landfill site on October 27, 1990. The mound on the left is nothing but chipped and shredded trees and other woody materials. Note the hood of a pickup truck at the far left of the picture. The mound on the right is composed of grass clippings, leaves and pine needles. All of these yard wastes were accumulated between September 1, 1990, and October 27, 1990, in this East Texas town of approximately 1900 people (about 900 households). Present plans are to let nature take its course and decompose these materials. Such a waste!

Picture #3
This is a bleak picture, figuratively and literally. Only this incinerator will be in operation after December 1, 1990, when Quitman's 5-acre landfill site will be closed. It is not expected that permission will be granted by the Texas Department of Health for this 5 acres of land to be used for any future purpose.

On November 21, 1990, I confirmed the above in a conversation with Mr. Bob Moseley, who is the Manager of Solid Waste Disposal for the city of Dallas. Mr. Moseley also told me, "This landfill's expected lifetime at *current disposal rates* is beyond the year 2040, or about another fifty years."

I really do not expect to live another fifty years, but my *children* could live that long. However, fifty years from now, my *grandchil-*

Picture #4
This is Dallas's McCommas Bluff landfill site on an overcast day in October 1990. Workers in the truck and trailer are readying some of our natural resources for burial in this dismal location. The wood shipping pallets shown on the right could have been used for a backyard gardener's compost bins!

dren will not yet be old enough to even begin thinking about retirement. I certainly do not want them to be burdened by the consequences of a *gigantic* landfill problem having been dumped on them by previous generations, including mine.

However, we need not be concerned about where the land for future landfill sites will be found, nor how many acres will be needed and how much the land will cost. We need to stop thinking of this as a *landfill problem* and start thinking of it as an *opportunity*. And now is the time to take action.

Stop sending your precious natural resources (grass clippings and leaves) to be buried in the landfill *now*. As you will learn from the following chapters, you will be greatly rewarded by recycling your grass clippings, leaves and some of your kitchen wastes.

The last chapter will explain how easy it is to recycle glass and

Picture #5

Just about all of the wastes shown above at the Dallas McCommas Bluff landfill location could have been recycled. The skyline of downtown Dallas is faintly discernible on the hazy horizon.

certain metal, plastic, and paper products, and how you will benefit from doing so. These four items account for over *half* of the volume of wastes being sent to the landfills each year.

Let me use Dallas as a reference in this regard one more time. If just *half* of the households in Dallas participate in recycling as outlined in this book, the Dallas landfill site will last *100* years. If most of the households participate, it could last much longer. And the same can be done in your community. (See Pictures #4 on Page 15 and #5 above.)

❖

CHAPTER 1

Why Compost?

If you were born and raised in a city and have lived in cities most of your life as I have, you may be asking, "What is compost?"

Instead of going into a long explanation at this time, let me give you a simple definition from the American Heritage Dictionary: Compost is "A mixture of decaying organic matter, such as leaves and manure, used as fertilizer." The compost you will learn to make from the information presented in this book will be made from your yard wastes, mainly leaves and grass clippings, and from your kitchen scraps and garbage. By "kitchen scraps" I mean such things as fresh vegetable trimmings, fruit peelings, stale bread, used tea bags, coffee grounds, etc. By "garbage" I mean leftover foods, cooked or not cooked, refrigerated or not, as long as the foods are not heavily saturated in oils or grease. I do not recommend putting meats of any kind in your compost piles. Neither do I recommend that you stop buying fertilizers as soon as you have learned to make compost.

You may now be wondering, "Well, the definition you gave me said it was used as a fertilizer. Is it a fertilizer or not?"

Compost will add nutrients to your soil, so it is a form of fertilizer. But, it is more than just a fertilizer. Think of it for now as a soil conditioner and fertilizer supplement when it is mixed into your soils. It is even more than that when it is also used as a mulch on top of your soils. Until you have added layers of well-enriched compost several inches thick for several years on top of your soil and then mixed them into your soil, you should continue using the same fertilizers you have been using. You will certainly not have to use as much of the other fertilizers once you begin using compost in this manner.

While we are on the subject of fertilizers and soil fertility, allow me to make a recommendation in this regard. The best way to find out just what your soil's fertility condition is, by far, to contact your state's nearest Agricultural Extension Service office and ask them to mail you a Soil Sample Kit. The kit you receive will furnish you with all the information you need about how to take the soil samples, the plastic bags in which you will put them, a list of the costs for the various types of analyses available to you, and mailing instructions. A few weeks after you mail your soil samples, depending on the time of year you are sending them, you will receive the information you requested along with recommendations on how to correct any deficiencies found.

In addition to the nitrogen (N), phosphorous (P), and potassium (K) levels, you will also be advised of the presence of, or lack of, several other major nutrients and some of the trace elements which are important to your soil's condition and to the health of your plants. For slight additional charges you can obtain a pH analysis, which informs you of the acidic or alkalinity condition of your soil, and an analysis which determines the percentage of organic matter in your soil.

So your next question might be, "If compost won't even keep me from having to buy other fertilizers, what *is* it good for?"

When compost is mixed into your soil, you will see an immediate improvement in the soil's structure, even if the compost is only partially decomposed. It will loosen compacted soils and provide air passages which will make more oxygen available to your plants' root systems. It will also hold water for a longer period of time in dry weather and improve drainage during wet weather.

When oxygen and moisture are available to soils containing compost, Mother Nature's soil microorganisms become energized, have a population explosion and further the decay of the compost, turning it into humus. The humus is what we want! It is the end product of our composting efforts. It is the humus which actually provides some of the plant's nutrients and improves the plant's ability to utilize other available nutrients. The humus content also regulates the soil's ability to both retain water and to release water excesses. It will provide sandy soils with improved water retention properties, yet it will improve drainage in clay soils. And after just a few years of incorporating compost into your soils, acidic soils will be less acidic and alkaline soils will be less alkaline. In other words, by annually mixing compost into your soils, to create humus, your soil's pH will tend to be neutralized. Fantastic!

Compost will also work wonders for you when you use it as a mulch to cover bare areas in your shrub or flower beds and in your vegetable garden. When used as an organic mulch, compost will help conserve water in several ways. It will slow down the surface evaporation which bare soils experience, keeping the soil moist for a longer period of time. The compost mulch will actually *hold* some of the moisture it receives and then slowly release the moisture as the soil begins to dry. It will also provide you with the same benefits which other more commonly used mulches do. It will stop the surface of your soil from crusting over, thereby reducing surface tension and soil erosion. If it is applied at least two or three inches deep, it will almost completely stop weed seeds and other unwanted seeds from germinating and taking moisture from the soil. Any such seeds which do germinate and finally stick their little leaflets above the compost mulch will be so weakened from this effort that you may easily remove them with very little effort on your part. Your compost mulch will act as an insulating blanket and will stop the quick, drastic soil temperature changes caused by extreme fluctuations in weather conditions.

All of the benefits derived from compost mulches mentioned above apply to shrub beds, flower beds, and vegetable gardens. Although it is unlikely such mulches would be tilled under in shrub or perennial flower areas (unless there is plenty of room between those plants), you *should* till the decaying compost mulch into your annual flower bed's soil and into your vacant vegetable garden's soil at the end of the growing season. This will stimulate the soil's microorganisms and they will more rapidly begin turning the partially decomposed compost into humus, readying the soil for your next plantings.

A beginning vegetable gardener may ask, "Are there any other uses for compost in my garden besides mixing it into the soil and using it as a mulch?"

Yes, there are many other ways to benefit from the use of compost. But first, let me recap what has already been covered. Your soil's structure will be less compacted and easier to work. Your plants' health will be improved by having more oxygen, having a more constant moisture level, being protected (when mulched) from extreme temperature changes, having better drainage, an improved pH, and an overall improved ability to utilize the available nutrients. Now, yes, there are more ways.

One of the best uses for compost is to provide a large shovel full of compost beneath the area where seeds are to be planted in hills. "Hills" is a horticultural term referring to the planting of a number of seeds, such as 5 or 6, close to each other with the intent of thinning out the unwanted seedlings a few weeks after their emergence.

The picture of cantaloupes (muskmelons) I grew last year in a four-foot by eight-foot raised bed is evidence of the results which can be obtained by using this planting method. *(See Picture #6 on Page 21.)* I planted one hill of the "Perlita" variety and one hill of a variety called "Magnum 45." After the seeds germinated and grew for a week or two, I removed all but two seedlings in each hill and then applied a compost mulch over the entire bed. Each hill produced over twenty cantaloupes which weighed between three and a half and four and a half pounds each, and the Magnum 45 variety presented me with two that weighed over five pounds. *(See Picture #7 on Page 22.)* Each melon was delicious, and while I am on this subject let me tell you something extremely important about growing cantaloupes. Do not give them any water during the last two or three weeks before time to harvest them. Excessive amounts of water when they are nearing maturity will ruin their sweetness. (I learned this the hard way the previous year.) I keep a nine foot by twelve foot plastic tarp close to my backyard garden and use it to cover my cantaloupe bed when rain is expected during this crucial period. One last bit of advice about growing cantaloupes or any other vegetable in your garden. Plant the varieties recommended for your area by your Extension Service.

This year I used compost in the same manner when planting my "Jack O' Hearts" (seedless) watermelon and had highly unusual and outstanding results. I had never tried planting seedless watermelons before. My curiosity and desire to plant them was aroused by Dr. Sam D. Cotner's article, "The Melon That's All Heart," which appeared in the March/April 1990 issue of *Texas Gardener* magazine. (Dr. Cotner is the Extension Horticulturist/ Project Supervisor, Texas Agricultural Extension Service, and au-

Picture #6
This prolific output of cantaloupe vines resulted from placing a shovel full of compost beneath the seed-planting area. After the seeds germinated, a compost mulch was used to cover the surrounding soil in the raised bed.

thor of *The Vegetable Book*, and *Container Vegetables* by Texas Gardener Press.)

I followed Dr. Cotner's planting instructions by starting my seedless watermelon plant in a peat pot and then transplanted it into my vegetable bed three weeks later. At that same time, two feet away in one direction I planted the pollinator watermelon seeds in a hill. (When you order seedless watermelon seeds, you

Picture #7

Two "Magnum 45" seedlings produced over twenty melons that weighed between 3-1/2 and 4-1/2 pounds each. The two shown above were the largest that were grown, and their flavor was wonderful.

also receive a seed package of an unknown variety to be used as a pollinator. At least, that is the way Porter & Son, Seedsmen of Stephenville, Texas supplied them.) Two feet away on the opposite side of my "Jack O' Hearts" seedling, I planted a hill of another self-pollinating variety named "Bush Jubillee." After the seedlings in the adjacent hills sprouted and produced their third set of leaves, I removed all but one seedling from each hill. What I wound up with was one pollinator variety on one side of the seedless variety and another pollinator on the opposite side of the seedless variety.

Now that I have explained the procedure which I followed, let me be more specific about exactly how the seedless variety was transplanted. I removed two shovels full of soil from the spot the seedling was to be planted, put one shovel full of compost in the bottom of the hole and then put a shovel full of soil on top of the compost. This area was then watered and gently firmed down. Then the remaining soil which had been removed was placed on top of the slightly depressed area, formed into a sloping mound, and lightly tamped. (In this case, the seedling was literally planted on top of a "hill.") I put a couple of handfuls of compost beneath the pollinators' hills before planting the seeds. All of this planting activity took place on May 13, 1990.

On August 7, 1990, the first ripe seedless watermelon was picked, refrigerated, and consumed. There were no black seeds and no large seeds found in the melon, only tiny white, immature, edible seeds. Between that time and September 23, 1990, twelve more seedless melons were picked as they matured, and there were fourteen more still on the vines in various stages of maturity. Four of the thirteen melons that were picked before September 23rd weighed between thirty and thirty-four pounds each, with the remainder averaging about twenty-five pounds each. Regardless of size, their taste was out of this world! *(See Pictures #8 and #9 on Page 24.)*

During the same time period mentioned above, six of the unknown (pollinator) variety had been picked with a total of six left on the vines, and the "Bush Jubillee" variety produced two good-sized melons. *(See Pictures #10 and #11 on Page 25.)* Each variety tasted very good, but I am now hooked on the "Jack O' Hearts"! It is a delicious melon and has no seeds which need to be picked or spit out.

Now, did this large shovel full of compost buried beneath the "Jack O'Hearts" melon cause this phenomenon? Did it also cause the extra large "Magnum 45" cantaloupes? I sincerely believe it did. This use of compost never ceases to amaze me. When compost was placed beneath tomato plants at the time they were transplanted into the garden, they also produced an abundant quantity with larger-than-normal fruit. It has worked for me on pepper, okra, and broccoli transplants.

So, in addition to just tilling compost into your vegetable garden and using it as a mulch, try this method of giving your transplants a little extra boost by putting compost beneath the planting spot. I am sure you will be rewarded as I have been.

And then you say, "Okay, you've got me convinced that compost is good for my garden soils, but can it be used in containers?"

You bet it can. More and more people who either have yards

Picture #8

These "Jack O' Hearts" seedless watermelons weighed over thirty pounds each. There were no black seeds to be concerned with when eating these melons.

Picture #9

Picture #10

These are 14 of the 27 "Jack O'Hearts" melons that came from one seedling transplanted above a shovel full of compost. The two "Bush Jubillee" melons are on the left and the six melons from the unknown variety (that were all pulled on the same day) are on the right. In the center of the picture below, the main stalk and root system of the "Jack O'Hearts" can be seen.

Picture #11

which are too small or too shady are growing flowers, vegetables, and even dwarf trees in containers, and they can certainly use compost mixed in with their potting soils. And, of course, there are also many who have plenty of space and plenty of sunshine who grow plants in containers outdoors as well as indoors. As you can imagine, the most commonly used containers range in size from relatively small six-inch pots up to fifteen gallon sizes or larger, depending on which plant, or plants will be grown in them.

I am sure there are many people who just use commercially prepared potting soils for their container plants. These work fine as long as correct watering and fertilizing procedures are followed. There are certainly some potting soils sold in plastic bags which are better than others and more expensive, also. My experience has been that "you get what you pay for" in regard to this, with one exception. You can buy the *least* expensive potting soil and improve it immensely by adding organic matter, especially compost, along with some good garden soil. Although I prefer to use compost, leaf mold can also be used to provide the necessary organic content. (How to make leaf mold is covered in Chapters 4, 5, and 8.)

Compost used in containers should not be that which you made in less than a month, nor that which you made in less than six months, unless you have allowed it to age or "cure" for a few weeks after removing it from the pile. And, compost should be "screened" before using it in containers smaller than a three-gallon size. (Chapter 3 will tell and show you how to screen compost.) When using unscreened compost in three-gallon or larger sized containers, I have had the best results when using a mix of one-third compost, one-third garden soil, and one-third inexpensive potting soil. I usually sprinkle in a few handfuls of perlite and vermiculite while combining these ingredients if the quality of the purchased potting soil is extremely poor.

I have used compost in this manner when growing tomatoes in seven-gallon containers and when growing lettuce and radishes in six-inch deep containers in my greenhouse during the winter months, and I have had healthy plants along with a good quantity of fresh vegetables all during the winter and early spring. *(See Picture #12 on Page 27.)* Although it is not absolutely necessary, I prefer to *screen* compost which is used as a *mulch* in all of my containers. The size of the particles, or texture of the screened

Picture #12

A "Patio" tomato plant (with a few ripe tomatoes) is in the center of the above picture which was taken in January 1989. A "Christmas Cactus" is in a hanging basket on the right of the tomato plant, and geraniums are on the left. This home-made greenhouse has only a small electric heater, and the plants are subjected to temperatures in the low forties when the outdoor temperatures are below 32 degrees (F). Compost in the containers and as a mulch help keep the plants healthy during these stressful periods.

compost, makes for a more attractive mulch and hastens the penetration of water into the growing media.

Our Alice Du Pont mandevilla was transplanted from a one-gallon container into a five-gallon container three years ago, using compost in this way. Since mandevillas are not cold-hardy here, I always cut the vines back to about two feet in height before the first frost each year and move the plant into the greenhouse. In late spring, after all danger of frost has passed, I remove the large bark nuggets from the surface of the container, apply about a one-inch layer of well-aged and screened compost and then put the bark nuggets back on top of this mulch. The container is then put

Picture #13

The Alice DuPont mandevilla blooms each year from May until the first frost is expected, which is usually in mid-November. Prior to the frost, the vines are cut off about two feet above the container, and the plant is put into the greenhouse for over-wintering. Compost helps all of the container grown plants make it through Texas' "dog days of summer" with flying colors. (Note that heavy duty shadecloth is stretched across the top of the greenhouse, and a light weight "Weed-Block" material hangs across the back windows to help provide protection from the late afternoon sun.)

outside, and she is ready to bloom all summer and fall again. *(See Picture #13 above.)*

Compost has been mixed into the soils and used as a mulch in all of our hanging baskets of annual flowers which get full sun, as well as the indoor hanging baskets of ivy and other greenery, with wonderful results. We have had the same experience with the large pots of Norfolk Island Pine and our Corn Plant (Dracaena Massangeana).

Another good use for compost is to incorporate it into the mix used in the bottom half of containers in which cuttings will be

Picture #14
The above foreground shows some of the author's plants that were rooted from cuttings in a potting mixture that included screened compost. Shown above are 4 Altheas (in different sized containers), 2 Asters on the far right, and 1 Camellia (behind the Asters).

rooted. It should be well-aged and screened when used for this purpose. Freshly made compost which has not fully decomposed will not burn the newly forming roots of the cuttings, but enough heat could be generated for awhile which might possibly delay their formation. And if an excessive amount of nitrogen fertilizer had been used when making the compost, this could also be detrimental. This is my reason for recommending compost being in the bottom half of containers in which cuttings are to be rooted. At that depth there is no way it can adversely effect the cutting's roots. On the other hand, once the roots grow enough to reach down into the compost, they will make optimum use of all the moisture and nutrients available to them, and the above-ground plant growth will thus be embellished. *(See Picture #14 on Page 29.)*

If you are in doubt as to the condition of the compost you plan to use in a container in regard to its being aged enough or in regard to its fertility, a good safety precaution would be to prepare the mix a few weeks ahead of time. From the time the mix is prepared until you are ready to begin rooting the cutting, you should have the mix in the container you plan to use and water it as though you were maintaining a growing plant. It would be a good idea to follow this method when transplanting from one container into the next larger size container if you are not certain of the compost's condition.

For my gardening friends here in Texas, I would be remiss if I failed to give you two excellent references for gardening in this area. *Neil Sperry's Complete Guide to Texas Gardening* explains how to cope with Texas's unique, diverse growing conditions and covers everything one needs to know about annuals, lawns, perennials, shrubs, trees, vegetables and a whole lot more. If your main interest is vegetable gardening, Dr. Sam Cotner's *The Vegetable Book—A Texan's Guide to Gardening* is a must for you. I never go through a gardening season without referring to it several times. I recommend it so highly and think so much of it that I do not refer to it by its title. I reverently call it, "The Vegetable Bible." Amen!

———————— ❖ ————————

CHAPTER 2

Just Enough Technical Stuff

People have been making compost for hundreds of years, using various methods to speed up the natural decaying process which takes place when plants die and fall to the ground. All organic matter eventually decomposes (even if left on top of the soil where it has collected) without any assistance from man. The decomposition of grass clippings and leaves which have fallen to a particular spot can be hastened considerably by merely raking and combining them into a pile and then letting Mother Nature do the rest. The composting process can be speeded up even more by mixing various types of organic matter, some green materials and some dried materials, for instance, before putting them into a pile. Adding cow or horse manures or some other fertilizers, along with some water, will result in a further acceleration of the decomposition. (These slow and not-so-slow methods will be covered in more detail in Chapter 7.)

During the 1930s, a British horticulturist by the name of Sir Albert Howard developed an improved method of making compost while he was doing research on this subject in Idore, India. His recommended method was to place a six inch layer of nitrogenous materials (grass, weeds, etc.) on the soil first. This layer was then covered with a couple of inches of manure and a sprinkling of soil, followed by a six inch layer of carbonaceous materials (dried leaves, hay, etc.) This layering of carbon and nitrogen materials, with manure and soil between each layer, was continued until the pile was five or six feet high.

Some authors of composting methods say Sir Albert's compost piles were six feet wide and ten to twenty feet long. Other authors have said the piles could be five feet wide and as long as you wanted them to be. I have also found that some said he recommended turning the pile twice at *three-week* intervals, and others reported he recommended turning the pile twice at *six-week* intervals. Anyway, they all agree he stressed the importance of moisture within the pile and a means of providing vertical air shafts or vent pipes through the center of the pile, and that such provisions assured usable compost after three months. And, the differences in pile sizes is not too disturbing, they would all decompose.

Since 1954, "Scientists in the Sanitary Engineering Department" of the University of California have been credited with developing what has been called the "14-day method" of making compost. I have read many gardening books and magazine articles written solely about composting and found a number of authors referring to this 14-day method in their writings. I have also found they had differences in opinions as to the validity of this method and discrepancies in exactly how the ingredients were prepared and combined.

Since I have been successfully making compost in three weeks or less for the past ten years, using a combination of Sir Albert Howard's method and what I could learn from various accounts of the 14-day method, these authors' differences and disagreements were not important to me. However, while writing this book, I felt obligated to find out as much as I could about the 14-day method. I finally was able to get in touch with Dr. Clarence G. Golueke who was one of the research biologists at the University of California involved in the development of this method.

On October 24, 1990, Dr. Golueke told me there was only *one other person* involved in this research which developed the 14-day method of making compost. This other person was a graduate student who completed his studies about the time the five thousand dollar budget for this research was depleted, and he left before the project was completed. In response to my questions, Dr. Golueke said there was no particular emphasis placed on the amounts of carbon- and nitrogen-furnishing organic materials used and no concern was given to the pH of the materials. The materials were not mixed together purposely before putting them into the 3' x 3' x 3' enclosure, although some combining may have occurred. Basically, the organic matter was put into the pile in a sandwich-type layering method as was done in Sir Albert Howard's method. Dr. Golueke also said it was not necessary to add large quantities of soil — at most just a few shovels full since the organic materials themselves contained enough microorganisms to start the decomposition process once they were provided with adequate moisture and oxygen.

Dr. Golueke confirmed that the key to success with this accelerated method was maintaining a constant moisture content, without a saturation of the materials, and frequent turnings of the compost pile to provide an abundant supply of oxygen. He said he turned the pile every third day (to accomplish both of these objectives) and "more frequently if the pile began to smell bad." In regard to the "14-day" reference he said, "Fourteen days was not a magic number. Actually it was a misnomer, a convenient term. Sometimes the pile was decomposed in fourteen days, and sometimes it would take seventeen days, eighteen days, or a day or two longer. Whatever was put into the pile decomposed. There was never a problem. Nature just seemed to take its course. Nothing but hand tools were used. The purpose of this research was to find an easy way for a backyard gardener to make compost, using simple hand tools, without taking up too much space and without taking so much time to make it."

And he did! What a pleasure it was to be able to talk to Dr. Golueke. He is a modest, likeable gentleman who is now seventy-nine years young. He is a professor emeritus, having retired as a faculty member of the Sanitary Engineering Division, Department of Civil Engineering, at the University of California at Berkeley, in 1978. He is presently a senior editor of *BioCycle* and is director of research and development in Cal Recovery Systems, a firm involved in the waste management industry. As we ended our conversation Dr. Golueke said, "Recycling is so important. I'm glad to see that composting is coming into vogue again." I believe he should be referred to as "Sir" Clarence Golueke!

MICROORGANISMS

No information about composting methods could be complete without a discussion of microorganisms and the part they play in the decomposition process. Although an understanding of some scientific principles may be of benefit, composting is not really a science; it is a form of art. In the composting theatre, the microorganisms are the *stars*. Without them no decomposition would take place—not in compost piles, not in forests, not anywhere. Without microorganisms, plants and animals could not live. And when they died, there would be no decaying, no rotting. Our *entire planet* would then become a *landfill,* and life on earth would cease to exist.

A science student offers, "Hey, I know a little bit about microorganisms. Are you talking about the microorganisms inside our bodies, or what?"

There are microorganisms in, and on, our bodies as well as plants, of course, but the relevent ones for this discussion are in our *soils.* They come in various shapes, and they are microscopic in size, naturally. Scientists have named them and they classify two of these groups of microbes as being either *aerobic* or *anaerobic.* The aerobic organisms live and work in an environment that has oxygen available to them. The anaerobic organisms live and work (at a much slower pace) in environments where there is little or *no oxygen.*

For purposes of future reference there are three other groups of microorganisms which scientists have appropriately named:

Psychrophile — "Psychro" is from a Greek word indicating "cold."

Mesophile — "Meso" is from another Greek word indicating "middle, center, or intermediate."

Thermophile — "Thermo" is from yet another Greek word that indicates "pertaining to or caused by heat."

The above definitions take care of the first two syllables of these terms, and the last syllable which is common to each group is "phile."

"Phile" indicates "one having love or strong affinity or preference for." "Phile" also comes from a Greek word meaning "beloved, dear, or loving."

So, thermophiles love it hot. Psychrophiles love it cold. Mesophiles love the middle range or mild temperatures. In other words, microorganisms can be counted on as being available to help break down the organic matter in compost piles, regardless of a pile's temperature. Of course, the thermophilic and mesophilic organisms work at much faster speeds than the psychrophilics. And, all of these microbes are in our soils all the time, no matter what the temperature is. For example, some of the thermophiles and mesophiles will die and some of them will go into dormancy when their soils become too cold for them. When the soil's temperature warms up to their liking, they break out of their dormant state and are ready to go to work when their other basic needs become available to them. Their other basic needs are water, food (organic matter) and, of course, oxygen for the aerobic microbes. When these basic requirements are provided, they multiply rapidly and greatly accelerate their rate of turning organic matter into humus.

The science student calls my hand again by asking, "Are microorganisms and microbes the same thing?"

Yes, they are. I should have explained that I will be using microbes, organisms, microorganisms and bacteria interchangeably. I may even throw in a few references to fungus and fungi, some of which are single cell bodies in the subkingdom of Thallophyta, but I promise not to get any more technical than that. As a wise old man once told me, "When you try to explain something, it is best to use the KISS method. Keep It Simple, Stupid."

Then the student says, "I understand what you have explained so far, but how many microorganisms are in average soils? Is there anything else I need to know about them?"

It appears the jury is still out, so to speak, in regard to the exact populations of soil microorganisms. Differences in soil textures and structures impact the quantities of such life in the soils. Temperatures of the soils and the availability of moisture, oxygen and organic matter greatly affects their numbers. For instance, there will be more such microbes found in soils from late spring through early fall, and the largest populations will be found close to growing plants and around decaying organic matter. To try to answer the question more specifically, J.S. Poindexter, in his book *Microbiology—An Introduction to Protists,* refers to estimates of "several million bacteria per gram of soil." Dorion Sagan and Lynn Margulis state, "No square centimeter of soil is free from bustling communities of *billions* of microbes," in their book entitled *Garden of Microbial Delights.* And, the *McGraw-Hill Encyclopedia of Science and Technology* is another excellent source for scientific information about microorganisms—the manner in which they promote plant growth, and their biological processes involved in the decomposition of organic matter.

There *is* just a little more necessary information about these little creatures. Some of the microorganisms in the soil prefer acidic conditions, some prefer alkaline conditions and some like neutral conditions. And of course, there are some which prefer organic matter that is high in carbon, others which prefer their diets to be high in nitrogen, and others which are not at all picky about what they have to eat. All groups have been called such things as "Nature's little composters," "Mother Nature's natural garbage disposers," and similar names. I have sometimes even referred to them as "little darlings" when putting a shovel full of soil into a compost pile.

pH

The beginning gardener then asks, "Is the pH scale that is used to express soil acidity and alkalinity the same as the one used to measure the pH of the water in my fish aquarium?"

All pH (potential of hydrogen) scales measure the acidity or alkalinity of a substance or solution, with readings of somewhere between 0 to 14, with 7.0 indicating the neutral point on the scale. The numbers below 7.0 indicate acidic conditions and the numbers above 7.0 indicate alkaline conditions. The more distant the numbers are from 7.0 in either direction, increasingly acidic or increasingly alkaline conditions are indicated. In other words, the highest number of the scale indicates extreme alkalinity and the lowest number indicates extreme acidity.

However, the pH scales which are provided with test kits for aquarium water and those used for testing soils differ greatly in their graduated ranges. Most aquarium water pH scales range from only a low (acidic) measurement of about 6.4 to a high (alkaline) reading of about 7.4. This is because water with a pH much below or much above this range will be detrimental to the health of the fish, particularly so on the acidic side. The pH scale is not a linear, but a logarithmic scale. For example, a pH of 5.8 is *ten times* more acidic than a pH of 6.8, and a reading of 8.2 would be *ten times* more alkaline than one of 7.2.

The pH scale used for *soil testing* is numbered in pH units from 0 to 14 (see next page), with the 7.0 neutral point meaning neither acidic nor alkaline conditions exist.

0	1	2	3	4	5	6	7	8	9	10	11	12	13	14

<— increasingly acidic <— | —> increasingly alkaline —>

Since the soil-testing pH scale is also logarithmic, a soil with a pH of 5.0 is *ten times* more acidic than a soil with a pH of 6.0, and a pH of 4.0 is *ten times* more acidic than a pH of 5.0 (or, *one hundred times* more acidic than a soil with a pH of 6.0!) The pH units on the alkaline side of the scale indicate increasing alkalinity in the same logarithmic fashion.

The pH of your soil is *one* of the environmental conditions which affects how well your vegetables and other plants will grow. Most vegetable plants will grow and provide their optimum harvests for you in pH ranges between 6.0 and 7.5, or, in other words, in soils that range from slightly acid to slightly alkaline. Either extremely acidic or extremely alkaline soils tend to tie up certain nutrients in the soils, making them either less available to the plants or not available at all. Such extreme conditions, of course, must be corrected to improve the health of the plants. Ground agricultural limestone can be used to correct strongly acidic soil conditions, and sulfur can be used to lower highly alkaline conditions. Depending on whether soils are sandy or heavy clay, which crops are to be grown, the organic matter content, and other environmental conditions, different amounts of lime (or sulfur) will be required to make these pH adjustments. And, such adjustments should be made gradually, just as they should be to correct the pH of aquarium water.

There are Soil Test kits and pH Analyzers available to you from mail order sources such as seed companies and gardening suppliers, and they can also be found at large nurseries. The Soil Test kits provide instructions, chemicals, color charts and paper for making a litmus test. The resulting color obtained from this test can be compared with the color chart to determine pH levels. The electronic pH Analyzers have a calibrated scale which gives a pH determination in less than a minute after inserting a probe (or probes) into moist soil. These kits and tools are generally reliable as far as giving an *indication* of the soil's pH condition. However, I believe a soil test should be made by your state's Extension Service every few years for comparison with such tests you have made to verify the accuracy of your testing procedures and equipment. If your soil's pH needs correcting based on their laboratory test, the Extension Service will include recommendations in regard to how to do this for *your* soil.

I do not recommend trying to adjust the pH of the organic matter which you are composting. You would only be "shooting in the dark" as to the outcome of such treatments, and you may do more harm than good. For instance, you may have read or heard that people with acidic soils should add lime to their compost piles so the compost will be alkaline and thus help make their soils less acidic when the compost is mixed into their soils. But, did they tell you exactly *how much* lime to add for the type of ingredients in your pile and for the volumes of those ingredients being used? And, although lime improves the texture of your finished compost, it also promotes a loss of nitrogen (by way of ammonium gas) as it increases the pH level of organic matter which is subjected to the high temperatures generated under aerobic composting conditions.

It is much better to give no concern whatsoever to your compost's pH level. Remember, after compost has been mixed into your soil for just a year or two, it will tend to neutralize the soil. If it then does not cause enough neutralization, as determined by an accurate soil test, *treat the soil. (See Picture #15 on Page 65.)*

C/N RATIOS

A person who has been making compost for a short period of time may be wondering, "What is the importance of carbon-to-nitrogen ratios which I have read about?"

All books and magazine articles which do a good job of explaining how to make compost emphasize the importance of using correct amounts of carbonaceous materials in relation to the amounts of nitrogenous materials being used. Many of these sources recommend a thirty-to-one carbon-to-nitrogen ratio (30:1 C/N), or thirty parts of carbon to one part of nitrogen, while others recommend a twenty-five-to-one ratio (25:1 C/N.) Recently I have read a few articles in which the authors stress the importance of using twice as much carbon materials as there are nitrogen materials being used. Would this be a 2:1 C/N? I am certain this is not the carbon to nitrogen *ratio* the authors are referring to, but rather, the quantities of materials, as you will see shortly. It is easy to understand how such differences in recommended C/N ratios could be confusing to a beginning composter.

In the same sequence as these ratios above were mentioned, let me assure you there is nothing wrong with a 30:1 C/N, nor is there anything wrong with a 25:1 C/N. This does not mean, however, that they were recommending using 30 (or 25) bushels of carbon materials for every *one* bushel of nitrogen materials. And, there is nothing wrong with using, for example, two bushels of dry leaves (carbon material) for each bushel of green grass clippings (nitrogen material), but this would *not* be a carbon-to-nitrogen ratio of 2:1. The following listing of the most commonly used composting materials, and the ranges in which their C/N ratios usually occur, can be used as a guide when putting together various ingredients for a compost pile.

ORGANIC MATERIALS	C/N RATIOS
Hay	10-25: 1
Kitchen scraps	15-25: 1
Grass Clippings	20-25: 1
Rotted manures	20-25: 1
Leaves	40-80: 1
Corn stalks	50-60: 1
Straws	50-80: 1
Pine needles	60-100: 1
Newspapers	150-200: 1
Sawdust	200-500: 1

The only purpose of the above list of various organic materials and their C/N ratios is to make you aware of the fact that certain organic materials are *extremely* high in carbon content. Newspapers and sawdust, for instance, and all woody materials (such as shrub branches, twigs, dried flower stalks, vines, etc.) have extra high C/N ratios. All such organic matter should only be used in small quantities, or not at all in compost piles desired to be *quickly decomposed.*

Since the largest number of homeowners interested in recycling their yard wastes have easy access mainly to grass clippings and leaves as ingredients for composting (or recycling by other methods which will be discussed later), let me use these two ingredients as an example of how to use the above information when wanting to make compost as fast as possible.

Equal amounts (by weight) of grass clippings with a C/N of 20:1 mixed with leaves having a 40:1 C/N *could* provide a combination averaging 30:1 (20 + 40 ÷ 2.) This combination of organic matter, in these proportions, has great potential for rapid decomposition. Grass clippings with the same carbon-to-nitrogen ratio (20:1) mixed with leaves having a C/N of 60:1 *could* furnish a combined average of 40:1 (20 + 60 ÷ 2.) This combination of ingredients is too high in carbon, in relation to the available nitrogen, and the microorganisms in a compost pile with this condition would readily use up the nitrogen before the carbon materials were decomposed. In this case, additional nitrogenous materials would have to be provided to correct this imbalance. The additional nitrogen can be supplied by more grass clippings being added to the mixture, by adding more than the normally used amount of fertilizers having a high nitrogen content, or by a combination of both.

The beginning composter may now be asking, "How do I *know* what the carbon-to-nitrogen ratio is of my grass clippings and my leaves?"

It is not necessary for you to know precisely what these ratios are. Grasses growing in soils in different parts of the country will of course vary in their C/N ratios. Not only do the soils differ, but the grasses differ, also. The same can be said for the differences in leaves, with some having a much higher carbon content than others, along with differences in acidity. Alfalfa hay and coastal bermuda hay differ in this regard also, as do different types of straw. If you really want to know what the C/N ratios are of your grass clippings and your leaves, you can send them to a laboratory to be tested, but this would be costly and totally unnecessary. I have made dozens of batches of compost with each batch taking three weeks or less to decompose using various kinds of materials: my grass clippings and leaves, different types of grass clippings and different kinds of leaves from my neighbors' yards, bales of spoiled hay given to me at a riding stable, and bales of straw I purchased at feed stores. There was very little difference in the amount of time it took different combinations of these materials to decompose even though the mixture of the proportions were about the same.

And finally, the beginner asks, "Why can't I just let my grass clippings decompose by themselves?"

You *can* just let your grass clippings decompose in a pile by themselves. However, grass clippings readily become matted and stuck together in a manner which does not allow oxygen to penetrate the pile. Since there would be a lack of oxygen, the fast-working aerobic microbes would be absent in such a pile and the slow-working anaerobic organisms, along with some earthworms, would slowly decompose it. (This slow method of composting will be covered in Chapter 7.)

However, do not be overly concerned about trying to get these C/N ratios exactly at 25:1 or 30:1. You do not have to make any arithmetical calculations! I guarantee that anyone who can physically turn a pile of compost every few days can make compost as fast as possible by using the recipes and following the instructions outlined in the next chapter.

FERTILIZERS

I prefer to use organic fertilizers when making compost or leaf mold because they are derived solely from the remains (or from by-products of the remains) of once-living organisms. They increase the microbial activity involved in the decomposition of organic matter by providing a source of protein for the microorganisms which the inorganic, man-made fertilizers do not. The organic fertilizer I use most often is cottonseed meal. It has a powdery texture which is light and easy to spread evenly, and it has a pleasant smell (especially when compared with the smell of synthetic fertilizers). Cottonseed meal is more readily available to plants in warm soils and is somewhat acidic in reaction, so it is a "natural" for the heavy black alkaline clay soils where I live. In other parts of the country, people making compost may prefer to use alfalfa meal, hoof and horn meal, blood meal, or animal manures.

All fertilizers, whether organic or inorganic, are labeled with three numbers which provide the percentage (by weight) of the three major nutrients in the container bag. These three numbers are referred to as the fertilizer *analysis* of the contents in the bag. The first of the three numbers represents the percentage of nitrogen (N), the middle number represents the percentage of phosphorus (P), and the last number represents the percentage of potassium (K). As an example, cottonseed meal has a NPK analysis of 7-3-2, and in a fifty pound bag there would be 3-1/2 pounds of nitrogen (7% of 50), 1-1/2 pounds of phosphorus (3% of 50), and 1 pound of potassium (2% of 50), or a total of 6 pounds of nutrients.

An inorganic fertilizer that is most commonly recommended for use on lawn grasses in my county has a NPK analysis of 15-5-10. A forty pound bag of this fertilizer would have 6 pounds of nitrogen (15% of 40), 2 pounds of phosphorus (5% of 40), and 4 pounds of potassium (10% of 40), or a total of 12 pounds of nutrients.

Both of the above mentioned fertilizers are also referred to as being *complete* fertilizers because they have *some* of each of the three major nutrients. There are many different formulations of synthetic fertilizers in addition to the 15-5-10, such as 16-4-8, 10-20-10, 5-10-5, etc., all of which are in the *complete* category. There are also many such fertilizers that have NPK analyses in which all three numbers are the same, such as, 10-10-10, 12-12-12, and 13-13-13. These are called *complete and balanced* fertilizers. And lastly, there are *incomplete* fertilizers such as ammonium sulfate, which has a 21-0-0 analysis, and super phosphate, which has a 0-20-0 analysis.

The table below gives cost comparisons between a fifty pound bag of cottonseed meal and a forty pound bag of the inorganic lawn fertilizer previously mentioned.

	15-5-10	Cottonseed Meal (7-3-2)
Total bag weight	40 lbs.	50 lbs.
Cost of bag	$6.00	$7.50
Cost per lb.	$0.15	$0.15
Total nutrients	12 lbs.	6 lbs.
Nutrients cost per lb.	$0.50	$1.25
Total nitrogen	6 lbs.	3.5 lbs.
Nitrogen cost per lb.	$1.00	$2.14

The prices shown for the bags of fertilizers above are the prices paid for them in the spring of 1990. The differences between the total weight of the bags and the total weight of the nutrients is the weight of the filler materials which are included in the bags to help spread, or broadcast, the fertilizers evenly. There are forty-four pounds of filler material in the fifty pound bag of cottonseed meal, and there are twenty-eight pounds of filler in the forty pound bag of 15-5-10. As can be seen, the cost per pound for the major nutrients, as well as the cost per pound of nitrogen in the bag of cottonseed meal, is more than double the cost for the same in the bag of 15-5-10.

A horticultural student then says, "You didn't give any cost comparisons for phosphorus and potassium. Why is that?"

Nitrogen was singled out in the cost analysis because it was *the* major nutrient with the highest percentage in each of the fertilizers. Also, most lawn grasses need fertilizers that are higher in nitrogen than in the other nutrients because most soils contain sufficient quantities of phosphorus and potassium. Although all three of these macronutrients are needed for maximum plant growth, nitrogen is used by plants in somewhat higher quantities, and it is leached from soils more readily than the other two nutrients.

The cottonseed meal which I use when making compost is, of course, also much higher in nitrogen content than in the other two macronutrients. This *natural* nitrogen source is consumed by the microorganisms most readily when the aerobic thermophiles and mesophiles are breaking down the organic matter in a compost pile or in soils.

A man-made fertilizer with a 15-5-10 NPK, instead of an organic fertilizer, *can* be used when making compost. As determined from the cost comparison table, two pounds of a 15-5-10 mixture would cost only thirty cents while four pounds of cottonseed meal (to provide the same amount of nitrogen) would cost sixty cents. As will be seen in the next chapter, this is approximately the amount of such fertilizers which would be used in a 3' by 3' by 3' (one cubic yard) pile of organic matter with a C/N in the neighborhood of 25:1 to 30:1. In other words, a cubic yard of grass clippings and leaves can be combined and *recycled* to provide the best possible soil amendment for either thirty, or sixty cents. And, it can be done right in your own back yard.

The same student then asks, "How much actual compost will I have after the pile decomposes and shrinks?"

After the cubic yard of grass and leaves is decomposed, the volume of compost will be about one-third of a cubic yard. In other words, it would take approximately three cubic yards of the materials initially in order to make one cubic yard of compost. This amount of compost could be made all at one time from a pile 9' long, 3' wide and 3' high or, three separate batches could be made from the previously mentioned 3' by 3' by 3' size. (A friend of mine paid $25.00 for one cubic yard of compost made by a business firm in the Dallas area this summer.)

While on this cost comparison subject, let me give another example of how money can be saved when purchasing fertilizers. Some of the commonly used inorganic fertilizers, such as 10-20-10 and 5-10-5, are packaged in the same weights and are sold for about the same price; however, notice the differences in the percentages of nutrients in the bags. The bag of 10-20-10 has *twice* the amount of the same three major nutrients than that which is in the bag of 5-10-5. The forty pound bag of 10-20-10 furnishes a total of 16 pounds of nutrients while the forty pound bag of 5-10-5 only provides a total of 8 pounds of nutrients. As an example, only twenty pounds of 10-20-10 would be needed to cover a thousand square feet of garden area at a rate of 2 lbs. per 100 sq. ft., but the *entire* forty pound bag of 5-10-5 would be needed to provide the same coverage.

And then the horticultural student says, "I know plants need *other* nutrients besides nitrogen, phosphorus and potassium. Can you tell me something about them?"

Before moving on to those other nutrients which plants require, a little more needs to be said about the importance of "The Big Three":

Nitrogen should be available to plants throughout their growing seasons since it is needed for plant growth. The frequency of application and the amounts required are dependent on the type of plants being grown and other cultural and environmental conditions. Nitrogen readily leaches from soils during periods of excess moisture, particularly in sandy soils lacking in organic matter.

Phosphorus can be thought of as a strengthening agent. It increases a plant's resistance to diseases and insect pests and provides the strength necessary for flowering, fruiting and the eventual maturing of seeds. It gives the plant's limbs and branches the strength to support heavy fruit crops. Phosphorus also promotes root growth to help support the plant. It is not readily leached from soils.

Potassium is renowned for contributing to the cold-hardiness of plants, yet it also increases plants' resistance to heat and diseases. It is involved in the photosynthesis process by which chlorophyll-containing cells convert light into chemical energy and in the formation of carbohydrates from carbon dioxide and water. Excessively high levels of potassium *inhibit* the plants' uptake of nitrogen. It is moderately leachable from soils.

There *are* many other nutrients which are needed by plants. Calcium, magnesium and sulfur, which are also macronutrients, are generally needed in relatively larger amounts than are trace elements such as, boron, cobalt, copper, iron, manganese, molybdenum and zinc. Calcium, magnesium and sulfur are not generally found to be deficient in most soils, and the trace elements (also called micronutrients) are needed only in minute quantities by most plants. Their availability to plants, however, is more adversely affected by abnormally low or high pH conditions than are the major nutrients.

In regard to making compost, none of the nutrients mentioned in the above paragraph need to be added to organic matter being composted. In fact, since grass clippings and leaves contain nitrogen, phosphorus, potassium, calcium, magnesium and even some of the trace elements, *no* fertilizer has to be added to these ingredients when making compost. However, my experience has been that the decomposition process can be speeded up by the addition of nitrogen, especially in an organic form such as cottonseed meal. It is a very inexpensive "treat" for the microorganisms, and they evidently have a great affinity for it.

An agricultural student then asks, "Can you tell me what the NPK analysis is for different kinds of farm animal manures?"

I *could* provide a list of the NPK analysis of various animal manures, such as cattle, horse and sheep manures, which I obtained from the Dallas County Extension office. But, unless you live in Dallas County, such a list would not be worth the paper it is typed on, and it could be misleading. Since the grasses, hays, straws and other foods these animals eat in different parts of the country have different nutrient values, so will their manures. Even the amount of moisture in the manures affects their NPK percentages.

The best advice I can give is for you to contact *your* County Extension office to obtain the nutrient values of animal manures in your geographical location. No matter where you live, though, you can use well-aged, rotted, or dried manures in your compost piles.

Let me emphasize a few key points worth remembering. When making compost using a method that provides an *aerobic environment* for the bacteria, the carbon-to-nitrogen ratios of the materials need to be *considered* in order to obtain the maximum decomposition rate. The C/N does not have to be 25:1 or 30:1, but should be fairly close to these ratios if you want to make compost as fast as possible. A compost pile that is built by alternately layering green grass clippings and brown (dry) leaves, as described in the next chapter, will provide an adequate C/N ratio.

It is important to know the pH of the soil and the soil's fertility level.

Plant's root systems cannot absorb soil nutrients unless moisture and oxygen are available in the soils.

Adequate amounts of organic matter incorporated into the soil (along with some extra nitrogen for the microbes) help improve the pH, the fertility level, the availability of moisture and oxygen, and the uptake of nutrients by the plants' root systems.

You can provide the ideal environment for the microorganisms in your soils by recycling your grass clippings and leaves, either by composting them before putting them into the soil, by using the grass and leaves as organic mulches, or by sheet composting, all of which will be explained in the following chapters. The "little darlings" will pay you back tenfold.

———————— ❖ ————————

CHAPTER 3

The Fastest Method

This fastest method of making compost makes optimum use of the heat generated initially by the mesophilic microorganisms, then by the thermophilic microorganisms, and then again by the mesophiles during the last few days of the decomposing process. Since both the thermophiles and the mesophiles are aerobic microbes, a constant supply of oxygen must be available for them. By frequently turning and aerating the organic matter, the person making the compost thus furnishes the needed oxygen. I sometimes refer to this method of making compost as the *aerobic* method, for two reasons: first, because the fastest-working microorganisms are *aerobes* and secondly, because the person who is turning the organic materials can get an *aerobic workout* while working fast at this operation. I mention this only to advise you that this method requires stooping, bending, reaching, lifting and even the shaking of the materials on the end of a garden fork during this turning procedure. When this activity is performed as quickly as possible, your heart beat will speed up, and so will your frequency of breathing. On the other hand, you can take your time and turn the pile at a pace that is more comfortable for you.

Even building the pile initially, lifting and dumping trash bags full of grass clippings and leaves or shoveling these materials from a wheelbarrow, requires a certain amount of physical exertion. This is why I recommend getting all of the ingredients ready to make the compost pile on the evening before the day the pile is to be built. In other words, mow the lawn, and bag the grass clippings, and shred the leaves (if this was not done before bagging them) on the evening before the pile-building day.

If you are not physically able or have no desire to perform the activities described above, please do not disregard the remainder of this chapter. An understanding of this fast method of composting will better your under-standing of the slower methods of making compost which will be explained in subsequent chapters.

However, before describing the actual combining of the ingredients, and certain other details involved in the preparation for this event, let me explain how closely this fast method of composting in an enclosure parallels what Mother Nature does when organic matter is blended into soils.

Grass clippings, shredded leaves, kitchen scraps and garbage can be mixed directly into soils at any time of the year, and they will be decomposed and turned into humus by the soil's microorganisms. They will be decomposed at a much *faster* rate, however, in *warm* soils than they will be in cold soils. The speed at which such organic matter decomposes in soils is greatly *reduced* in *excessively wet* soil conditions, due to insufficient amounts of *oxygen* being available to the aerobic microorganisms. And if the carbon-to-nitrogen ratio is high, as is the case with leaves, for instance, the microorganisms will use some of the soil's available *nitrogen* during their decomposing activities, unless some kind of high nitrogen fertilizer is added to the soils.

When we humans combine the *right kinds* and *amounts* of organic matter in an enclosure and *maintain* the right amounts of *moisture* and *oxygen* therein, we are providing an ideal controlled environment for the "microscopic composters" to do their work. The "little darlings" will begin to work so fast that they will generate the *warm* temperatures which the mesophiles like, who then will have a population explosion and then more of them will work even faster than before and generate the *hot* temperatures which allow the thermophiles to multiply and thus generate even *hotter* temperatures. If, when we first combine these ingredients, we provide a carbon-to-nitrogen ratio that is too high, the microbes will use up the available *nitrogen* and we will need to provide a nitrogen supplement to the pile. This nitrogen supplement can either be in the form of green grass clippings, other nitrogenous materials, or a high nitrogen fertilizer.

Later in this chapter I will explain how to approximate the quantities of the different types of organic matter being used, ascertain the availability of moisture and oxygen in the pile, determine whether or not the C/N ratio is within bounds, and show

how a thermometer is invaluable in monitoring the conditions within the pile. These explanations will be given under headings entitled **Building The Pile, Turning The Pile,** and **Monitoring The Pile.** But, before we begin to build a pile, a few things must be made ready beforehand.

ENCLOSURES

Since the least amount of organic matter required for this fastest method of composting is a cubic yard in volume, an enclosure (or bin) that is at least three feet long, three feet wide, and three feet high can contain this amount of materials. The vertical sides of the enclosure will allow all of the ingredients for the pile to be uniformly three feet in depth from top to bottom. If space is available for larger enclosures in which more compost can be made at one time, bins that are four feet long, four feet wide, and three feet high can contain forty-eight cubic feet of materials (compared with the twenty-seven cubic feet in the 3' by 3' by 3' enclosures). If an enclosure is not used and the materials are merely combined and formed into a sloping mound on the ground, those ingredients in the lower half of the inclined surface will not be piled deep enough to allow the desired amount of heat to be generated and maintained.

Bins made for fast composting can be made in various shapes and sizes as long as they can accomodate at least a cubic yard of materials and have the proper depth. As will be seen shortly, they can be made out of different kinds of wood, concrete blocks, bricks, or concrete reinforcing wire, and they can be made inexpensively if so desired.

Five years ago I was able to obtain 10 wooden (oak) shipping pallets at a very reasonable price from a store that was going out of business. To form these pallets into a 3-bin arrangement, I first put 3 of the pallets end-to-end close to, and parallel with our cedar fence and bolted the ends of the pallets together. Since these pallets are 48" x 48" square, this provided a length of about twelve feet. Next, the ends of four other pallets were secured to the first 3 pallets at right angles to them, with 1 pallet at each outside end, and 1 at each end of the pallet in the middle. This provided three equal sized spaces along the twelve foot run. The remaining 3 pallets were then placed across the front of the three U-shaped openings and they were secured to the ends of the 4 pallets only with screen door hooks so that they can be easily removed when turning the piles. *(See Picture #16 on Page 66.)*

The manner in which wooden pallets are made allows air to circulate into the enclosure from all directions; however, the spaces between the horizontal boards is too wide to prevent the organic materials from falling (or being thrown) through them when turning the pile. One-inch mesh chicken wire was stapled to the inside-facing boards of each pallet to prevent the materials from falling out. For reference purposes when explaining the turning procedure, the bin on the left will be referred to as bin #1, and the bin in the middle will be referred to as bin #2. The bin on the right (bin #3) is used only for storing compost for later use.

All composting ingredients should have some kind of a cover to protect the organic matter from rain. Either clear plastic sheets, or black plastic sheets, or trash bags can be put on top of the organic materials. The plastic coverings will have to be weighted down with rocks or pieces of wood around the edges to prevent strong winds from blowing the plastic cover off. An old water hose can also be used to form a circular weight over the top of the plastic. Or a cover can be made out of light-weight framing wood, covered with fiberglass as *shown in Picture #16 on Page 66.*

This three-bin arrangement for composting is handy, but it is not a necessity. Seven such pallets can be used to make a two-bin arrangement for alternate use in turning the piles. Storage of excess compost or compost desired to be aged for awhile can be accomodated by plastic bags or other containers.

Even a *two-bin* arrangement is not necessary. Just a single collapsible bin will suffice. For instance, four pallets formed into an upright square and only secured end-to-end with screen door hooks or latches or just tied together with wire will work fine. When the time comes to turn the pile, unhook (or untie) the pallets. The pile will stay in place while the pallets are put back together adjacent to it. Then start turning the pile into the enclosure.

If inexpensive shipping pallets are not available and you do not want to spend much money on a compost bin, wooden frames can be made from 2" x 4" lumber made into 3' by 3' squares, and chicken wire or hog wire can be stapled on the inside of the square frame to form a suitable enclosure for the organic materials. As mentioned above, four of these square frames could be used for a collapsible bin, or seven frames could be made into a two-bin arrangement. A bin for storing of excess compost can be added whenever it is needed. Again, if space for the bins is not a limiting factor, make the frames larger so more compost can be made at one time. Lumber treated with boiled linseed oil will withstand the high humidity and heat generated in composting enclosures better than untreated wood.

An inexpensive yet perfectly satisfactory enclosure can be made out of two 10' pieces of 3/4" electrical conduit. Cut the conduit in half so there will be four 5' pieces to serve as the corner posts. Measure off a 4' by 4' square on the ground and drive one of the pieces of conduit into the ground at each of the four corners of the square. They should be driven into the ground at least a foot deep. If the ground is dry and hard, pour a little water around the conduit as it is being driven into the soil. Then use chicken wire, or almost any kind of wire mesh, to enclose the area. This sixteen square feet of enclosed ground area will accommodate forty-eight cubic feet of organic matter when it is piled three feet high. When the pile needs turning, remove the wire mesh, and two of the pieces of conduit. Drive these two conduit pipes into the ground four feet away from the pile on the opposite side, forming another four-foot square for the pile. Put the wire mesh around the four pipes again and turn the composting materials into the new enclosure.

A piece of concrete reinforcing wire mesh, cut three feet in width and twelve feet long, can be formed into a circular enclosure with a diameter of about 3-1/2'. A cubic yard of organic materials can be placed into this round enclosure. When the pile needs turning, untie the ends of the wire, remove it from the pile and form it into a circle next to the pile, and so on.

At the opposite end of the compost enclosure spectrum would be bins that can be made as elaborate and attractive as can be imagined. Concrete blocks or bricks can be used to form the U-shaped walls of the enclosure with attractive gates or doors on hinges across the front to provide access to the piles. There should be a space of about one inch between each brick (or concrete block) to provide the necessary air circulation within the bins. Ornamental iron posts such as those used to support carport or patio covers can be set in concrete at each end of the enclosure to support a roof over the area. This covering will protect the pile from rain and also protect the composter from direct sunlight in the heat of summer.

Another attractive configuration can be made by setting 4" by 4" by 8' cedar posts in concrete to support a roof over the enclosure. Horizontal 1" by 6" (and as long as needed) cedar boards can be secured to the posts to form the U-shaped bins. (There should be about one inch of horizontal air space between the boards.) The front can be enclosed by the same boards, either in the form of a gate or in a slotting arrangement which allows the boards to be removed one at a time for access to the pile.

As can be seen from the foregoing, there are no strict rules about designing an enclosure for this fast method of composting as long as the bins will accommodate at least a cubic yard of organic matter of the proper depth. The depth of the materials being composted does not have to be three feet unless the width and length of the bin are each only three feet (thus providing twenty-seven cubic feet of enclosure). For example, the inside dimensions of the bins formed by my 48" square wooden pallets are 42" by 42", and I have made many batches of compost by using this fast method when starting with a pile of organic matter that was only thirty inches in depth. (This 42" by 42" by 30" volume equates to thirty cubic feet, or slightly more than one cubic yard.) The high temperatures were reached just as quickly and maintained just as long at a thirty-inch depth as they were at a depth of three feet, and the decomposition of the materials occurred in the same amount of time.

GRASS CLIPPINGS

I normally follow the recommendations of my local Extension Service in regard to mowing my bermuda grass lawn. I mow the lawn every 5 or 6 days so that only one-third of the leaf surface is removed at any one time, and I let the grass clippings fall and be recycled and decomposed by Mother Nature right there in the lawn. (More will be said about this method of lawn mowing in Chapter 8.) When I want enough grass clippings for a new batch of compost, I let the grass grow a few days longer between mowings so the clippings can be bagged for this purpose.

Since some of my neighbors have not yet started composting,

and they do not recycle their grass clippings in their lawns, I occasionally will get some of their bagged grass clippings for my compost piles. I always find out from them how long it has been since "weed-killers" (such as "MSMA") were sprayed on their lawns before taking their grass clippings. If it has been at least three weeks, the residual from such spraying will have dissipated. In addition, the blades of grass on which the poison was sprayed will have been watered several times, and the grass will have grown and been cut several times during this three-week period. If a more potent weed-killer had been applied, I will not use their grass clippings but will instead wait a few days longer and use my own clippings.

The ideal time to mow the lawn and collect clippings for a compost pile is immediately before making the pile. By doing this, the fresh green clippings will not have had time to become matted or stuck together in the plastic bags. However, in the heat of summer, it is quite an unpleasant task to mow the lawn and build a compost pile which involves lifting bags of grass clippings and bags of shredded leaves (which were left over from the winter) combining them, etc.

In my younger days, I used to do this all at one time, usually on Saturdays. Now that I am older (and wiser), I mow the lawn and bag the clippings on the evening before the day I plan to start building the compost pile. In this way, the fresh grass clippings will still be loose and easy to spread when I need them. The next morning, just as the sun begins to rise, I start combining the ingredients for this *fast method* of composting, but *I* do not have to work fast while doing this work. All of the necessary ingredients are piled next to the compost bin, a water hose is handy, the early morning temperature is mild, my favorite mockingbird usually starts singing while perched at the top of a nearby power pole, and this endeavor becomes an enjoyable pastime. It only takes about an hour of time (and no perspiration) to build a pile in this manner.

LEAVES, HAY, OR STRAW

About the time trees start dropping their leaves in the fall, the grass-mowing season comes to a halt. Here in North Central Texas, I can usually collect enough grass clippings either from my yard or from my neighbors' yards to make one more pile of compost as the leaves begin to accumulate in sufficient quantities. This is the time also to collect as many leaves as possible for shredding and saving for the next year's compost piles. Of course, many more leaves can be packed into plastic bags or other containers if they are first shredded. In addition to storing leaves in plastic bags in out-of-the-way places, leaves can be put into empty compost bins and covered, or they can be piled up into mounds and covered in a corner of the yard.

There are many other uses for leaves in the fall and winter months. They can be shredded and used as a mulch in shrub beds, tilled into vacant vegetable gardens, or they can be used for making leaf mold. All of these uses for leaves will be explained in the following chapters.

If your property does not have enough large trees to supply you with leaves to be used as mentioned previously, you can probably locate all the leaves you want by driving around your neighborhood or an older neighborhood that has plenty of large trees. The leaves may already be in plastic bags, waiting to be picked up and delivered to the landfill for burial unless you get to them first.

When the weather warms up the following year and fresh grass clippings again become available, the leaves that were saved for making compost in the summer will probably not be in sufficient quantity to make more than a few fast batches of compost. Many times in the summertime, I have gone to heavily wooded public parks where leaves were still lying all over the ground from the previous winter. In less than an hour, enough leaves can be bagged for a compost pile or two in a situation like this. And, some of the leaves will have already begun to decompose.

Bales of hay or bales of straw may be substituted for leaves when making compost. Riding stables and boarding stables almost always have bales of spoiled hay which cannot be fed to the horses. Spoiled hay readily decomposes when mixed with fresh grass clippings at about the same ratios as previously mentioned for leaves, and most owners of these stables will usually give the spoiled hay to you just for the asking. Suburban feed stores sell bales of fresh hay and bales of straw, also. One bale of either hay or straw will be enough to furnish the needed carbon (when mixed with green grass clippings) for two compost piles in bins that will accomodate one cubic yard of these materials.

SHREDDING

It is not absolutely necessary that leaves be shredded for this quick method of composting, but they will be slightly more decomposed than whole leaves will be at the end of this fast composting cycle. An inexpensive yet very good method of shredding leaves is to put them into a thirty or forty-gallon trash can, filling the can only about halfway to the top with leaves. Then use either an electric or gasoline weed trimmer to shred the leaves inside the container. The leaves will be sufficiently shredded in *less than a minute.* Then halfway fill the can with more leaves and shred them with the line trimmer. This procedure can be repeated several times until the volume of shredded leaves is about halfway to the top of the container. Then empty the shredded leaves from the container and start over with more leaves. My small (10" diameter) electrically powered trimmer does a better job of shredding leaves with the *guard removed.* However, do not use a trimmer in this manner unless safety glasses are worn because small twigs or woody leaf stems can occasionally be thrown upward and out of the container. This is also the reason for not filling the can more than halfway with leaves. *(See Pictures #17 and #18 on Pages 67 and 68.)*

A lawn mower with a bagging attachment does a good enough job of shredding leaves. And if the leaves are scattered all over the lawn, the grass is being mowed at the same time the leaves are being shredded. A mower without a bagger can also be used for shredding leaves. Just rake the leaves into small piles in an area where the mower's discharge of the shredded leaves will be accumulated, such as against a garage wall, wooden fence, or in the proximity of the compost bins.

Another method of collecting and shredding leaves that I like is to use the vacuum attachment on my gasoline powered leaf "blower-vac." The leaves are torn apart as they are being vacuumed into the tube and discharged into the attached heavy duty cloth bag. If I want the shredded leaves in a plastic bag or other container, I hang the blower-vac from its handle on a hook beneath the support beam of the carport cover, place the container beneath the suspended bag, open the zipper and empty the leaves into the container below. *(See Picture #19 on Page 69).* Or if shredded leaves are needed in a compost bin, the blower-vac can be held in an upright position (with one hand) on top of one of the sides of the enclosure, with the bag hanging down into the bin, and the leaves can then be emptied.

Electric blower-vacs work just as well and cost only about half as much as the gasoline models. There are, of course, many other types of leaf-eaters, shredders and chippers which can be used for shredding leaves, in prices ranging from about $100.00 and up.

KITCHEN SCRAPS AND GARBAGE

Depending on the size of the family and the family members' eating habits, kitchen scraps and unwanted leftover foods should be saved for a number of days prior to the pile-building day. A container with a tight-fitting lid is good for this purpose, with the size of the container dictated by the expected quantities of wastes to be accumulated. Or relatively small quantities can be put into a plastic bag and kept in the refrigerator until they are to be used. I have found it to be impossible to save too much of these wastes for a new compost pile! But remember, no meats, fats, or oils should be included.

Kitchen wastes should also be saved and put into the compost pile each time the pile is being turned. Previous additions of these wastes will not be found during subsequent turnings of an actively working pile. I recently put fifteen dozen chopped bananas into a compost pile during the second turning of the pile. When turning the pile four days later, not a single identifiable piece of banana could be found. However, I do not recommend putting huge amounts of kitchen wastes into a pile during the last (usually the fourth) turning, unless the pile will then be left undisturbed for at least a week.

VENT PIPES

Sir Albert Howard was the composting pioneer who first recommended the use of some kind of an air shaft or perforated pipe placed vertically through the center of a compost pile so that oxygen would be available in the middle of the pile, thus helping to speed up the decomposition of the organic matter. He also was the first to recommend the sandwich-type layering of the organic materials (with alternating layers of nitrogenous materials and carbonaceous materials) and the need for moisture within the pile.

A four-foot length of plastic drain pipe with 1/2" holes drilled through the pipe about every six inches in all directions throughout the length of the pipe makes an excellent vent pipe for a compost pile. The heavy duty plastic drain pipe (called a "schedule 40" pipe) which I have been using for ten years on a regular basis, looks as good now as it did the first time it was put into a compost pile. It will evidently last forever, being impervious to high temperature, humidity, and stress. When building a compost pile for the first time on dry, hard soil, dampen the area in the center of the bin and tap the top of the pipe with a hammer until it will stand vertically on the wet ground. The first layer or two of organic matter is then placed somewhat snugly against the pipe. From that point on, there should be no problem with the pipe tending to lean. If it does, just make it vertical again and pile more organic matter around it. If this same spot of ground is used frequently for compost piles, there will be no need to tap the pipe into the soil when first placing it. The soil will be so soft that the pipe can be pressed into it by hand. A satisfactory substitute for a plastic pipe can be made out of concrete reinforcing wire mesh. Cut a piece of this wire mesh one foot wide and four feet long and form it into a four-foot tube-shaped cylinder.

THERMOMETERS

I have been using thermometers to monitor the increasing and decreasing heat levels of compost being made by this fast method for about nine years. I am not sure how I got started using the thermometer, but I must have read that someone recommended it shortly after I began using this accelerated method of composting. If the originator of this idea was known to me, I would certainly want to acknowledge his (or her) contribution. A thermometer is as necessary for this method of making compost as a stethoscope is to a nurse or a doctor.

For the first few years, I used a thermometer that is normally used for testing the temperature of candy or other liquids being boiled in the kitchen. That thermometer was encased in a glass tube that was about 1/2" in diameter and about six or eight inches long. It worked very well until I accidently broke it one day while turning the pile with a garden fork. The one I have been using since that time is in an aluminum casing that is about a foot long, and it has a round, red plastic ball secured to the end that protrudes from the top of the compost pile. As I recall, Santa Claus ordered this one for me from a mail order gardening supply place. I believe it cost almost twenty dollars, but it is worth every penny. It should last at least as long as my schedule 40 vent pipe will.

As previously mentioned, "Sir" Clarence G. Golueke was the research biologist who developed the 14-day method of composting at the University of California at Berkeley. In my conversation with him in November of 1990, he told me that the compost piles on which he did his work were actually located about 8 miles off-campus at the university's Richmond Field Station. The compost piles he built were in hand-made enclosures which were located inside a shed. He said that the reason that the minimum size for the enclosure for composting organic materials by this greatly accelerated method was 3' x 3' x 3' was because he found it took about a cubic yard of these materials in order for the microorganisms to generate a sufficient amount of heat, and for the heat to be maintained for several days, since this volume of materials had the characteristic of being self-insulating. And lastly, this size of an enclosure would not take up too much room in a homeowner's back yard, and the pile would not be too cumbersome for the average person to work.

In my opinion, "Sir" Clarence G. Golueke should have been raised to knighthood for his pioneering accomplishment in the field of composting. Never before, in the history of composting, have so many owed so much to one man. At least, that is the way I see it.

BUILDING THE PILE

A compost bin that has inside dimensions of 42" by 42" by 42" will require twelve 32-gallon plastic bags full of organic matter to fill the 1-1/2 cubic yard area of the bin. Six such bags full of fresh green grass clippings and six bags of shredded and packed leaves is a favorite recipe of mine and it has never failed to make compost in less than three weeks. Most of the time, my work on the pile is completed on the sixteenth day (the day on which I turned the pile for the fourth time). On a few occasions, I have either gotten the ingredients too wet or did not get them wet enough, and this added two or three days to the length of time it took for the microbes to finish their work. On those occasions I also had to do a little more work because the pile had to be turned to either help it dry out or to add the necessary moisture.

Freshly cut green grass clippings have a certain amount of moisture in them, and if they are packed into plastic trash bags and left in the bags too long, they will become matted or stuck together. When such bags are emptied into the bin, a garden fork or other tool will have to be used to loosen them so that oxygen can penetrate into as much of the clippings as possible. However, even though the clippings inherently have moisture, additional moisture must be added to the pile to compensate for the dryness of the leaves. Similarly, shredded leaves that appeared to be dry at the time they were put into plastic bags can absorb a certain amount of moisture from condensation within the bag if they are kept in the bags for a lengthy period. When the bag of leaves is emptied into the bin on top of the layer of grass clippings, the leaves must also be fluffed and loosened and, ideally, somewhat mixed-in with the grass clippings. Even if the leaves that were at the bottom of the bag are *sopping* wet, additional water will have to be added to the pile.

As can be seen, estimating the correct amount of water to be added to the compost pile is somewhat of a challenge. I experimented on two different piles started a few years ago. Each pile had the same kinds and quantities of ingredients (grass clippings and leaves) and when the first pile was completed, the next one was built immediately. These piles were built during the hottest part of the summer in my area, July and August. I *measured* the amount of water that was put into the piles as they were being built, by filling one-gallon jugs from a water hose whenever I wanted to add the water. In the first pile, twenty-five gallons of water were used while building the pile initially. I used twenty gallons of water while combining the ingredients for the second pile. Each pile was made into compost in less than three weeks, and each pile reached and maintained the desired temperatures during the first four days. On the fourth day, the piles were turned and water was added. Each time the piles were turned after that, a little water was added. All of which brings up this next point. No two compost piles can be built exactly the same. Even if *scales* are used to weigh each bag of ingredients, there will be differences in the amounts and types of nutrients (as well as the amounts of moisture) in different bags of the same kind of organic matter. Therefore, measuring the amount of water used when building a pile is not the solution, although the amounts so used can be a guide for future piles. The next few paragraphs will explain how best to add water and how to determine when the ingredients have been sufficiently moistened.

Before putting the first bag of organic matter into the compost bin, first water the soil within the enclosure. If that soil has been unused for a period of time, or if it is completely dry, it will tend to soak up too much moisture from the initially placed ingredients. And by wetting the soil, the microbes in the top few inches of the soil will be more readily aroused when the organic materials are placed on top of the soil. After the soil has been wetted, stand the vent pipe vertically in the center of the area and begin putting the first bag of grass clippings into the bin. When the 32-gallon bag of clippings is emptied, spread the clippings evenly over the top of the soil. Be sure to fluff them if they are at all matted or bound together. Then add about half of one of the bags of leaves and scatter the leaves over the entire surface of the grass clippings. Using a garden fork, aerate the leaves and work them into the grass clippings. Now add water, either from a fine spraying hose, or from a sprinkling can. About a gallon of water, evenly distributed over the mixture, should be sufficient. Then use the garden fork's tines to lightly scratch around within the mixture, thus furthering the dampening of the leaves. If they appear to be dry, sprinkle more water. Then add the remainder of the bag of leaves and spread a small shovel of loose soil over them, along with four or five handfulls of cottonseed meal sprinkled over the top of the soil. Then again sprinkle about a gallon of water over the top of the mixture and combine into the mix with the garden fork. While stirring and scratching the top few inches of the mix with the fork's tines, look closely at the moisture content of the pile. The dry matter, or leaves, should glisten slightly if they are damp. The reason for only putting half of the bag full of leaves into the pile at one time and for scratching the surface of the pile after mixing with water is to slightly dampen all of the leaves. If all of the leaves in the bag are dumped into the pile at once, it is more difficult to moisten them. If you can liken the consistency of the mixture to that of a wet sponge which has been thoroughly wrung out, the amount of moisture should be about right. If the ingredients appear to be too wet, with water standing on the surface, for instance, add a shovel or two full of dry soil. That completes the first two layers of this twelve-layer "cake."

Now put another layer of grass clippings on the pile. *(See Picture #20 on Page 70.)* Spread and aerate the clippings as before, and then cover them with half of a bag of leaves. Sprinkle the leaves with water, lightly mix the leaves into the clippings, add sprinklings of soil, fertilizer, and water. Take another close look at the moisture of the pile and be guided accordingly.

After the next layer of grass clippings and a layer of leaves are added to the pile, begin adding the kitchen wastes to the pile. Depending on the amount of such wastes, they may can all be added at once when the pile has reached half of what the height will be of the finished pile. Spread the kitchen wastes evenly over the surface of the center layer of the pile. If a large volume of these wastes is available, only put about half of them on this center layer and put the remainder on top of the next layer of clippings and leaves.

Continue alternately layering clippings and leaves as outlined above until all of the organic ingredients have been added to the pile. When all of the ingredients for building a pile such as this are prepared ahead of time, the actual building of the pile as described above takes about an hour. *(See Picture #21 on Page 71.)*

Insert a thermometer into the pile approximately six inches from the edge of the vent pipe. A screwdriver with a long shank, or a similar tool, should be used to open a hole in the organic matter so the thermometer can be easily inserted to its maximum depth. Now cover the top surface of the pile with a few of the emptied plastic bags and weight them down, even if there is a solid cover above the enclosure to prevent rain from soaking the pile. Plenty of air can get to the pile from all sides of the pile and by way of the vent pipe in the center of the pile. The purpose of the plastic bag placement is to reduce evaporation from the top of the pile and to help the pile heat up quickly. Twenty-four hours after finishing the pile, check the pile's temperature. The thermometer should indicate a reading of between 120° (F) and 160° (F). (Mine average reading about 140° (F) on the first day after building a pile.) If a reading in this range is obtained, everything in the pile is in good order at this time. Place the thermometer back in the same hole from which it was removed and make a written record of its reading for future reference. The location of the thermometer does not have to be exactly six inches from the edge of the vent pipe. It can be twelve inches from the pipe, and the temperature will be the same. However, if it is placed just a few inches from the outside edge of the materials, the reading will be much less and therefore unreliable. Close to the center of the pile is where the action is, and that is what needs to be monitored. So get in the habit of placing the thermometer in about the same location all the time. Also take and record a reading about the same time of day every day. This is the only sure way of knowing what kind of microbiological activity is taking place in the pile. For several years now, a friendly neighbor occasionally greets me by asking, "Well, Dr. Whitehead, have you taken your patient's temperature today?" I always answer affirmatively. *(See Picture #22 on Page 72.)*

All of the above and the following narrative pertain to compost piles which are built during the time of year when green grass clippings are available naturally. In other words, ambient temperatures do have an effect on the ability of the pile to heat up to the desired temperature and to be able to sustain these temperatures within the pile. However, I have started such piles in the middle of October with nightly outside temperatures in the forties, and the piles were decomposed by the middle of November. When the grass clippings are no longer available, Mother Nature provides the falling leaves for us, and we can put them to good use, also.

Continuing with the scenario of the just-built compost pile, the temperature will normally rise again on the second day, or just drop slightly, and on the third and fourth days it will continue to drop. On the fourth day, the pile should be turned to add oxygen and water for the aerobic organisms.

If the pile does not heat up twenty-four hours after it is built, or if it does not heat up to the above mentioned temperatures by the second day after it is built, something is wrong within the pile. If there is an unpleasant aroma coming from the pile, the ingredients are *too wet*. This condition can correct itself (if not totally saturated) in a couple of days. Removing the plastic bags from the top of the pile and punching holes in the top of the pile may help it to recover sooner. If you want to make compost as fast as possible, however, the best way to correct this condition is to turn and aerate the pile. If the pile does not heat up, and if it does not smell bad, it did not have *enough* water to begin with, or there is a shortage of nitrogen, or both. In this case, the pile must be turned so that adequate amounts of water and/or nitrogen can be provided within the pile. And lastly, if the pile heats up satisfactorily the day after it is built but the temperature then drops drastically (fifteen degrees or more) on the second day, this is also a signal there is an insufficient amount of water in the pile and the pile must be turned so water can be added. It is not likely that there is a shortage of nitrogen in this case since the pile heated up on the first day, but it is possible. The importance of using a thermometer when making compost by this fast method should now be easily understood. You do not need a thermometer unless you want to recycle your yard and kitchen wastes as fast as possible.

TURNING THE PILE

Before explaining the steps to take under normal turning conditions (when the pile heated properly and maintained temperatures above 140° (F) for a few days), let me explain how to correct the problems mentioned in the above paragraph.

If the pile did not heat up and there was a foul odor coming from it, the anaerobic (no oxygen) microbes have inhabited the pile due to excessive moisture conditions. Remove the front part of the bin so access to the pile is gained, remove the thermometer and plastic cover, and remove the vent pipe from the center of the pile and stand it up in the adjacent empty bin. Then use a garden fork and begin forking the materials from the pile. While doing so, be constantly mindful of the work in progress or why this work is having to be done, and do everything possible to loosen up the saturated matter so as much air as possible can enter the ingredients. If this is being done during the hottest part of the summer, it is best to do this work as early as possible in the morning or during the last hour of sunlight in the evening. (This is for the benefit of the compos*ter.*) When a forkful of wet matter is removed from the pile, it should be thrown up into the air slightly and into the adjacent bin. After several forkfuls have been so deposited, step over to their new location and slash and tear them apart with the ends of the fork tines. Then reach around the sides and back edges of the saturated pile with the fork and get some of this drier matter every so often and put it into the center of the new pile. Then get some more of the wet stuff and toss it onto the new pile. Continue this slashing and tearing apart procedure, and every now and then scoop some of the material off the new pile and bounce it up and down on the ends of the tines. When the materials in the new pile are about a foot in depth, spread a few shovels full of dry soil over the pile and continue this procedure until all of the organic matter has been turned into the new enclosure. If there is no chance of rain, do not put the plastic covering on top of the pile but do put the thermometer back in place. There should be *some* build up of heat after about twenty-four hours, but it may take a couple of days for the desired temperatures to be reached, depending on how wet the pile had been and how good a job was done in aerating it. I have only had to turn an excessively wet pile twice in the last seven or eight years, and I do not expect to ever do it again. I cannot remember hearing the mockingbird sing while I was performing *this* task. It was not an enjoyable pastime.

Now let me explain how to analyze and correct another type of problem with a compost pile that does not heat up properly. If there is no heat in the pile and the pile does not smell bad, the pile is *not* too wet. Either the pile is lacking in moisture content, or there is not enough nitrogen in the pile in relation to the amount of carbonaceous materials. I have never encountered the latter situation, evidently because the correct amounts of grass clippings have been mixed with the correct amounts of leaves, and cotton-seed meal has also been added to each pile. A pile that is too dry is much easier to turn than one that is too wet. The weight of the materials is much lighter and easier to turn. But again, remember why this effort is having to be expended and look closely at the condition of the organic matter while in the process of turning it. The leaves will not be glistening and the grass clippings will have begun to dry out somewhat. Take the time to moisten the pile after every three or four inches of materials have accumulated in the new enclosure, but do not get the pile *too* wet.

The solution to the problem of a pile heating up properly the day after it is built and then experiencing a drastic drop in tem-

— continued on page 81 —

Picture #15
Thanks to annual additions of compost, the author's heavy black (alkaline) clay soils have a neutral pH.

Picture #16

The fiberglass cover is raised when work is to be done in bin #2 or bin #3. A three-quarter inch plywood cover, painted red on one side and white on the other side, only partially protects bin #1 from rain, so plastic bags are needed to cover the compost when it is in this bin.

Picture #17

A "compost can" whose bottom has been removed can be temporarily taken off
its compost pile and used as a container for the shredding of leaves. Turn the
can upside down, slip a plastic trash bag over the small end of the can and then
turn the can up as shown. Fill the can only about halfway with the leaves to be
shredded.

Picture #18

In less than a minute, even a small electric line-trimmer can do an outstanding job of shredding leaves in a can. Since the trimmer's guard is removed for this procedure, safety glasses are worn when using it. Be sure the guard is put back onto the trimmer before using it for edging, trimming, or for other uses.

Picture #19

The vacuum attachment shreds leaves as they are sucked into the tube and then collected in the attached bag. Emptying the shredded leaves is made easy by suspending the blower-vac above a container and then opening the bag's zipper.

Picture #20

This shows a new compost pile being started in bin #1. Note that all of the required ingredients are close at hand. In addition to the bags full of grass clippings and shredded leaves, also shown is a colander full of kitchen scraps, a container of cottonseed meal (with red lid), a small plastic bag full of kitchen wastes next to the cottonseed meal, a watering hose and some of the "tools of the trade."

Picture #21

The depth of this new compost pile in bin #1 is about thirty inches. Two shovels full of finished compost taken from bin #3 are spread over the top of the new pile to provide additional microorganisms to speed up the decomposition of the organic matter. Soil can be used instead of the compost, but if compost from a previous pile is available, use it. (There will, for certain, be *billions* of microorganisms in just one large shovel full of compost.)

Picture #22
The red plastic ball is the thermometer's "flagged" location. A plastic covering is put around the "oxygen tube" in the pile and over the entire top surface of the compost to help the pile to heat up and to reduce the amount of moisture loss caused by evaporation. The "patient is now put to bed."

Picture #23

The grayish-white areas denote the presence of fungi at work. A steamy vapor arises from a sufficiently heated pile when the pile is being turned.

Picture #24
While turning the pile from bin #1 into bin #2, the author shakes and bounces the composting ingredients into the air in order to provide an abundant supply of oxygen for the aerobic microorganisms.

Picture #25
The first turning of the compost pile (into bin #2) is now completed. All available kitchen scraps, along with a sprinkling of cottonseed meal and water, are added each time a pile is turned.

Picture #26
A 2" by 4" by 48" piece of lumber is placed across the opening above the pile and used as a "chopping block" for kitchen scraps being added while in the process of turning the pile into bin #1. (Do not keep any fingers close to the chopping block when the machete is descending upon it.) A light sprinkling of cottonseed meal is then added and watered down before covering the kitchen scraps with a few more inches of composting materials.

Picture #27

After the second turning of the pile, the compost is again in bin #1. The height of the pile is only slightly lower than it was when it was first built due to the fluffing of the organic matter during the turning operation.

Picture #28
The composting ingredients are noticeably darker in color after they are turned for the third time, and they are now again in bin #2. The continued reduction in the height of the pile is additional evidence of decomposition.

Picture #29

After the pile is turned for the fourth (and last) time, the vent pipe is removed, the pile is leveled and then allowed to cool a few days before the compost is used. What had been a cubic yard of organic materials just 16 days ago has now been decomposed into one-third of a cubic yard.

Picture #32

"Black gold" is obtained from the sifting of compost through a one-half inch wire mesh screen made for this purpose. (The prospector's hands are those of the author's wife.) The screened compost now has a sweet, clean, earthy smell and it crumbles easily. The large pieces of compost which do not go through the screen are either put back into the storage bin for further decomposition, or used in the garden.

perature the following day, is the same as was explained in the preceeding paragraph. As far back as I can remember, I have only had to turn piles twice due to their being too dry when they were put together. The first time or two you build a compost pile for this fast method, it may be well for you to review the section on **Building The Pile.** I hope my relating of the experiences I have had will help you avoid these pitfalls.

Now an explanation of the procedures involved in the turning of a pile under *normal* conditions is in order. In other words, the pile is now ninety-six hours old, and it has performed admirably for this length of time.

My experience has been that compost piles which have been built with the right combination of ingredients (including moisture) will *always* heat up to 130° – 150° (F) within twenty-four hours after they are built. Most of the time, the temperature will continue to climb the following day, sometimes reaching 160° (F). On the third day there will be a drop of between five and ten degrees, and a similar drop in temperature will occur on the fourth day.

The pile's decreasing temperatures are signalling that the interior portions of the pile are experiencing a decrease in the availability of moisture and/or oxygen. In either case, the pile needs to be turned in order for us to provide these requirements for continued fast decomposition. In addition, the exterior portions of the pile have not been subjected to the high temperatures, as were the ingredients in the center of the pile.

When turning the pile, a concentrated effort must be made to put all of the organic matter which is in the outer six-inch thickness (around all sides of the pile) into the middle portion of the new pile. This is, of course, so that the outer ingredients can be exposed to the highest temperatures, which will speed up their decomposition. And since temperatures of at least 140° (F) will kill weed seeds and grass seeds, as well as many of the disease-causing bacterium (pathogens), we want *all* ingredients of the pile to experience these high temperatures for at least one day.

Moisten the soil in the area into which the pile will be turned, and remove the vent pipe from the pile and stand it up in the center of the new bin location. Remove the plastic covering and the thermometer from the pile, and begin removing the materials from the top of the pile first. As these composting ingredients are being placed into the new pile's area, fluff them as much as possible by bouncing them up and down on the garden fork's tines while holding the fork parallel to the surface of the soil. Let the ingredients fall through the air a few feet while scattering them onto the moistened soil below.

Then begin removing the materials from the outer edges of the pile. These materials will be the driest of all the matter in the pile, and they will be lighter and easier to separate and thus easier to aerate than the decaying ingredients in the center of the pile. They will also require more water to get them properly moistened, and they should be sprinkled with water before they are covered with any of the ingredients from the middle of the pile. Some gray powdery looking areas may be seen in some of the outer (dry) layers of the pile. This is of no concern; it is probably just fungi working at a slow pace, and the condition will be corrected when these parts of the pile are put into the middle of the new pile.

As additional organic matter is removed from the top and then from the middle of the original pile, there is usually a certain amount of steam arising from the pile as more and more of the center's ingredients are exposed to the fresh air. Accompanying this vapor will be the smell of ammonia that is being released by the nitrogen-containing organic matter. (There is a characteristic odor to this ammonia aroma, but it is not a pleasant one.) However, this is a good sign of the condition of the pile. It is an indication that there was still some nitrogen available to continue the breaking down of the organic matter. And usually at about the same depth in the pile where this condition is found, there will also be some light gray moldy-looking patches of matter. There is nothing wrong with this condition either. These gray areas are usually quite moist and are only a sign of anaerobic activity or a different breed of fungi. These areas will be particularly benefited by the turning and aerating of the pile. *(See Pictures #23 and #24 on Pages 73 and 74.)*

When removing the organic matter from the center of the pile, much of the matter will still be somewhat moist and will tend to cling together. These clods must be torn apart and opened so that oxygen can be made available. Lift them and turn them upside down, slash at them with the fork's tines turned sideways, and then scoop them up and hold the fork's tines flat and horizontal while they are bounced in the air and allowed to fall onto the new pile. The microorganisms will not be hurt by this vigorous activity. They will instead be helped by having more oxygen being made available to them.

Each time the middle area of the old pile's height is reduced several inches, stop removing the organic matter from the middle and resume removing the matter from around the outer edges. Again, observe the condition of these ingredients and add moisture to them after they have been fluffed and put into the middle of the new pile. Add available kitchen wastes to the new pile in the same manner this was done when the pile was built.

Continue these same procedures until all of the original pile's ingredients have been aerated and formed into a new pile. The reason for turning the pile in this manner is to provide an abundant supply of oxygen throughout the pile, to be able to check the moisture condition of the organic matter, and to provide the water that is needed. Be careful not to add too much water, which would necessitate turning of the pile again within the next day or two. The first time a pile is turned and thoroughly aerated and fluffed in the manner just described, the height of the newly turned pile will be about the same as it was when the pile was originally built. *(See Picture #25 on Page 75.)* After this first turning, the pile will shrink in size during the next four days, and then it will need to be turned again. It takes about the same amount of time to turn a compost pile the first time as it took to build the pile, or about an hour. When completed, insert the thermometer in the same general location as before, and cover the pile. (My friendly neighbor refers to this as "putting the patient to bed.")

Assuming the pile was aerated properly and the moisture needs were attended to when the pile was turned, there should be a build up of heat within the pile before the next twenty-four hours have passed. The temperature should be within a few degrees of what it was twenty-four hours after the pile was first built. By reading the temperature every day for the next four days at approximately the same time, the temperature fluctuations will be seen to follow the same pattern as was recorded during the original four-day period. Normally, the temperatures will again reach, or be above, the desired 140° (F) reading for a day or two. If this level is not attained, it may be due to the moisture content of the pile or the pile is running out of nitrogen. There is no cause for alarm, however, if the temperature is at least above 130° (F) because the microbes are still working at a fairly good clip. If the temperature drops below this level, the pile needs to be turned. Otherwise, wait until the fourth day to turn the pile for the second time.

While turning the pile the second time, the same critical attention needs to be given to the oxygen and moisture provisions as was previously given when turning the pile. If there is not an ample supply of kitchen wastes to be mixed into the pile, it is usually a good idea (and maybe an ounce or two of prevention) to sprinkle two or three handfuls of a high nitrogen organic fertilizer over the ingredients as they are being turned and watered. This should be done about three times as the pile continues to increase in height. This is particularly important if the organic matter being turned does not appear to be either too wet, or too dry. If a large quantity of "tough" leaves (such as oak leaves) were used when building the pile and the leaves were not shredded, the microbes may have just about used up the pile's nitrogen by this period of time. Oak leaves have a reputation for being difficult to decompose, but I have not had a problem with decomposing shredded oak leaves when using my "combustion chamber" method of fast composting, if adequate amounts of nitrogen are provided. After completely turning the pile, place the thermometer in it and cover the pile as before. Again, there will be very little difference between the height of this aerated and fluffed pile and the height of the pile after it was turned for the first time. (See Pictures #26 and #27 on Pages 76 and 77.) It usually takes about ten or fifteen minutes less time to turn the pile on the second turning.

Again assuming all is well within the pile, a build up of heat will be noted twenty-four hours after the pile was completely turned. Occasionally, there will be a continued increase of the heat within the pile on the second day after it was turned. (This will most often occur when nitrogen fertilizers or large quantities of kitchen wastes are added to the pile while it is being turned.) After the second day of heat build up, the temperature will drop on the succeeding days. When four days from the last turning have elapsed, it is time to turn the pile for the third time.

During the third turning of the pile, a difference in both the texture and the color of the ingredients will be noticeable. Small parts of leaves will still be distinguishable throughout the pile as a rule, and some chunks of grass clippings will also still be identifiable. Tear the chunks apart during this turning operation and moisten them if they appear to be dry. The majority of the organic matter will have begun to darken in color, and some of it may be in small round shapes about the size and color of horse manure. Again, be mindful of the moisture content of the materials and also fluff them so there will be easy access for oxygen. Add kitchen wastes or a light sprinkling of fertilizer in the middle of the pile, as done during the previous turnings. After the third turning is completed, some shrinkage of the height of the pile will be in evidence. It will usually be about three-fourths of a cubic yard in volume. When the turning is completed, place the thermometer in and the plastic covering over the pile. This third turning usually will require between thirty and forty minutes to complete. *(See Picture #28 on Page 78.)*

Continue to monitor the pile's temperature every day and record the readings each day during the next four days. The temperature readings during this period will normally average from a high of about 140° (F) to a low of about 125° (F).

On the fourth day after the pile has been turned for the third time (the sixteenth day from when the pile was built) the pile will be turned for the last time.

As mentioned previously, I prefer to do this type of activity early of a morning as soon as there is enough light to be able to see the pile's ingredients while they are being turned. It is again necessary to be cautious in regard to aerating the organic matter and in providing water for the microbes because *they* have not yet finished *their* work. I believe it was over-confidence that caused me to be neglectful one time when I over-watered a compost at this stage in the pile's life. That time, however, the over-watering only caused a few days' postponement of the "ready" date for using the compost. I knew it was not necessary to turn the pile anymore since it had been turned three times previously and all of the ingredients had been exposed to high enough temperatures. However, when the microorganisms are provided the necessary oxygen, water, and "vitamins" (organic fertilizer) during this fourth turning, the pile's temperatures will usually be only slightly lower than they were after the third turning. The "peak" temperature is always less than the previous highs, but the range will usually be from about 130° (F) to about 115° (F) for two, three, or four days.

I do not recommend putting large quantities of kitchen wastes into the pile at this time. For example I would not put a gross of chopped bananas into the pile, but a dozen chopped bananas would be decomposed quite readily. The reason for this is that some of the thermophilic organisms will have died and left the remainder of the decomposition work to be done by the mesophilic organisms. (When the "little darlings" died, the nutrients which their tiny bodies had consumed were released back into the composting organic matter.) The mesophiles are rather fast workers also, however, and they are additionally stimulated by this availability of nutrients and will quite fastidiously complete the decomposition of the organic matter. When their work is completed, there will be a significant temperature drop to about 85° (F) and their population will likewise be greatly diminished. Those which survive, in conjunction with the increasing psychrophilic population, will continue to decompose the pile. At this time, however, the vent pipe is removed from the pile and the pile is leveled and left in place for another day or two, at which time the compost can be stored for future use, or used immediately as a mulch, or it may be tilled into vacant soil areas. *(See Picture #29 on Page 79.)*

As indicated above, the compost is now usable. It will not have a fine texture at this stage, but it is finished compost in this sense; no additional turnings of the pile, nor additions of nitrogen, will cause the pile to heat up again. The pile has decomposed by the assistance of man as much as it can be decomposed. After a few days, the compost can then be screened. It will be dark in color, finely textured, and it will have a clean, earthy fragrance after it is screened. Truly, it is then "black gold."

An attentive, patient, beginning composter then asks, "Why do you recommend turning the piles every four days instead of every three days like "Sir" Golueke did?"

Good question. Until I spoke with "Sir" Clarence G. Golueke, I understood from my readings of various accounts of his 14-day method that either three or four days was the proper amount of time to be allowed between turnings of the piles. I have had experience only with turning the piles every four days, and since that is my only first-hand knowledge, that is all I can honestly relate to you. My compost piles have always been completed between sixteen and twenty-one days, and that is really not much longer than what "Sir"

Clarence G. Golueke found with some of his compost piles. However, when the grass turns green next year and the fresh clippings become available again, I *will* try turning the piles every three days, and you can try it, too. I am absolutely certain it will work.

And then the beginning composter asks, "Why do you recommend recording the daily temperature readings of the compost piles?"

This is probably because I sometimes have trouble remembering from one day to the next, but I will explain more about this in the following section.

MONITORING THE PILE

Allow me to re-emphasize the following. In order to keep abreast of the decomposition activity taking place within the compost pile, the temperature readings should be taken at approximately the same time of day, every day. I habitually do this around seven o'clock each morning and a little earlier than this on the fourth day after the pile was turned. On the fourth day I want to take the pile's temperature as soon as there is enough light in the sky for me to be able to take the reading and before the rising sun begins to heat up the environment in which I will be working.

During five months of the year, from early March through late July, in addition to the singing of my favorite mockingbird, I am able to hear the happy "chirp, chirp, chirpping" of my purple martins as they glide to, and fly from their nests. Many times, they will perch on their porch railings and sing to me while I am tending to the compost business. *(See Picture #30 on Page 89.)* When the martins leave their nests and begin their migratory flight to Brazil (and after I make certain they have departed for this destination), I clean their living quarters and use their nesting materials in my next compost pile.

The reason I recommend that the beginning composter keep a record of the daily temperature readings is so the composter can quickly become familiar with the desired temperature fluctuations (the "peaks and valleys") that are normal within a compost pile being made by this fast composting method. By keeping a record of what occurred within the first pile (temperature-wise), the composter will have a guide, or pattern to which the progress of the second pile may be compared. Do not expect to see the exact same temperatures recorded from one pile to the next, but do expect to see similar peaks and valleys in approximately the same temperature ranges for every pile made by this method. I kept such records of every compost pile I made by this method for several years and actually charted them on graphs. I still jot down the daily readings in my planning guide-calendar.

In July of 1990, I was asked if I would give a presentation about some of my composting methods at the October meeting of the Dallas County Master Gardener Association. In preparation for the presentation, I referred to the daily temperature readings recorded during the making of a compost pile by this fast method and made a chart from that record. A picture of the chart was then taken, and it was used as one of the colored slides shown during the "How to Compost" presentation, along with a few other such charts for comparison purposes. A picture is worth at least a thousand words. *(See Picture #31 on Page 89.)*

Now let me recap some of the characteristics of the "goings-on" of a compost pile that is made by this fast method, while discussing the temperature chart of such a pile *(Picture #31)*. All temperature measurements refer, of course, to the Fahrenheit scale. The amounts of grass clippings, leaves, etc., used for starting this pile are shown on the chart.

One day after this pile was built, the temperature reading was 142°, and on day #2 the reading was 151°. (Sometimes the reverse will happen, with a much higher temperature being recorded on the first day.) On day #3 the temperature dropped ten degrees, and another ten degree drop was noted on day #4. This is the indication that the microorganisms need more air or more water or both.

Kitchen wastes and water were added to the pile while it was being turned and aerated on day #4. The temperature reached 150° on day #5; then it dropped to 148° on day #6, to 145° on day #7, and to 140° on day #8.

The same ingredients as above were added while turning the pile on day #8. The next day, the temperature was recorded at 146°, and on the 10th day the reading was 144°. On day #11 the temperature dipped below 140° for the first time, falling to 137°, and it continued to drop to 132° on the 12th day.

While turning the pile for the third time (on day #12), a cottonseed meal "vitamin shot" was administered to the pile, along with the food and water. The inhabitants within the pile responded

Picture #30
The purple martins seem to enjoy watching humans work in the garden close to
their living quarters. They also appreciate shredded leaves, grass clippings and
small amounts of loose hay being available for their nest-building activities.

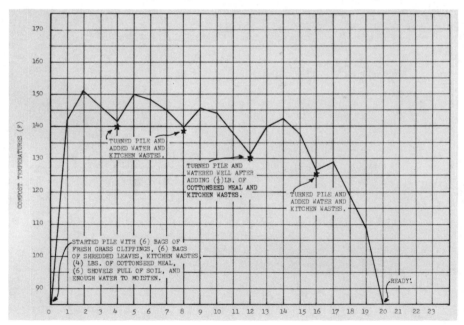

Picture #31
A chart made from the daily recordings of the compost pile's temperature
readings can be used as a reference for, or comparison with, the performance
of future piles.

well and caused the pile's temperature to climb to 140° the next day and on up to 143° on the 14th day. The temperature then dropped sixteen degrees during the next two days, falling to 127° on day #16. This sixteen degree drop in a two-day period at this stage is a signal that many of the thermophiles have deceased, and the surviving ones are slowing down their activities. It is also an indication that the organic matter in the pile has been mostly decomposed at this time and little, if any, increase of temperature will be realized as a result of turning the pile for the fourth time. (But I usually turn it anyway.)

On the sixteenth day, the pile was turned for the fourth (and last) time. The temperature only climbed two degrees after the pile was turned (even though water and kitchen scraps were added) and it then fell more than forty degrees during the next three days. The mesophilic organisms became active during this period of time, and the size of the pile was noticeably reduced.

As indicated above, it was not necessary to turn the pile for the fourth time. I could have just let the temperature continue to fall, and the pile could have been ready a couple of days sooner. But, there were some kitchen scraps available, I had the time (it only took about thirty minutes to turn the pile), and I needed the exercise. Besides that, I believe I derive some therapeutic benefits from this activity.

About the only thing that will keep me from turning a compost pile when it needs to be turned, is rain. The pile would get too wet, even in a sprinkling rain and the decomposition process would slow down considerably and the pile would smell bad. Maybe...one of these days I will build a shed over the compost enclosures...there could be a skylight in the roof...it could have movable slanted slats beneath the opening...tools and bagged leaves could be stored...and hay...and...I may just build it next spring.

SCREENING

One of the definitions of "screen" is, "to separate or sift out by means of a sieve or screen." And that is what screening compost does, allowing only small particles of compost to pass through the screen while trapping the larger pieces of compost above the screen. The size of the particles screened will vary, depending on the size of the openings in the wire mesh used for this purpose.

A popular size for such a screen is made out of one-half inch hardware cloth stapled to a wooden frame that fits the dimensions of the top edge of a wheelbarrow's bed. A trowel, small shovel, or a small piece of 2" by 4" lumber can be used to rake over the compost placed on top of the screen, and to force the small particles through the screen. After screening the "black gold" through the wire mesh and into the container below, the larger pieces of compost which resisted this effort can be put into storage for further decomposition or put into the garden. *(See Picture #32 on Page 80.)*

While building a workbench inside my greenhouse, I fixed part of the workbench's top so it could be raised, and then framed a built-in (but removable) one-quarter inch hardware cloth screen below the top surface of the workbench. A plastic tub can be placed and removed below the screening area of the workbench to collect this more finely screened "black gold" for use in seedling containers. This smaller mesh screen is also used for screening out the large pieces of "timber" which are sometimes found in bags of inexpensive potting soils. *(See Picture #33 on Page 92.)*

A vegetable gardener then asks, "Did you say you put screened compost into containers used for growing seedlings?"

Yes, screened compost is an ideal ingredient to be mixed into the medium which will be used for growing seedlings. It is not particularly helpful to put screened compost into seed-starting trays from which small seedlings will be removed because the seedlings will only be in the trays for a short period of time, and they do not need this extra nourishment at this initial growth stage. But do add compost to the mix into which the seedlings will be transplanted. They will love it.

A person who is several years my junior then says, "I have to leave the house at daybreak to go to work, and I do not get home until after sundown. How can I make compost by a fast method?"

Compost can be made in exactly the same manner, as described previously in this chapter, by turning the pile once a week instead of every four days. The rate of decomposition will not be as fast, naturally, but if the pile is attended to properly each time it is turned, it will be decomposed in about six weeks. By the time the pile is turned on Saturdays, for example, the temperature will have dropped into the 130° to 120° range because by that time the moisture and oxygen will have been mostly depleted. During the intervals between the turnings of the pile, it will be helpful to punch vertical holes down into the pile with something like a crowbar and occasionally pour water into the holes. Making the size of the pile larger will help, also. Make the bin 3' high, 3' deep, and 6' long and then place two vent pipes, two feet apart in the center of the enclosure. This area will accomodate twice the volume of a 3' by 3' by 3' bin, and the pile will be somewhat more efficient in its self-insulating ability. If this 3' by 3' by 6' pile is turned properly every weekend, it will be decomposed in six weeks, and it will provide twice as much compost as would the smaller size.

The amount of compost a homeowner can make each year is limited only by the availability of yard wastes and the homeowner's desire and willingness to make the compost.

As you will see in the following chapters, there are many other methods of composting. And, although composting is a biological process which decomposes organic matter in a controlled environment, it is impossible for you to not be successful. If all of the needed ingredients were available, you could have built a cubic yard pile in about the time that it took you to read this chapter.

Picture #33
A one-quarter inch wire mesh screen provides "black gold dust" to be used in containers for transplanted seedlings. The "gold dust" is collected from a removable plastic tub beneath the screen. Any pieces of compost which do not go through the screen are used as a mulch for plants growing in containers.

CHAPTER 4

The Compost Can Method

Almost everyone can make compost by the compost can method. It is ideal for people who have small yards with limited quantities of yard wastes and for those who are not physically able to handle large amounts of organic matter as described in the previous chapter. However, those who have enough yard wastes and the ability to make compost by the fast method can also make compost by the compost can method at the same time. During the summertime, I normally make compost using both of these methods, plus the Tumbler Method, all at the same time. It just seems impossible to make enough of this wonderful stuff.

Either a plastic or metal trash can may be used as a container for this method. A 32-gallon size container will do fine, but if a larger one is available, such as a 45-gallon size, more compost can be made at one time with very little extra effort. Whether the can is plastic or metal is a matter of choice, but be advised that the bottom of the can will have to be cut out and removed and holes will have to be drilled into the can and into the can's lid to allow air into the organic matter. I have one plastic and one metal container that I use for the compost can method. Each can is a 32-gallon size, and I drilled about one hundred holes into each can. The holes are spaced about four inches apart in a checkerboard pattern completely around the circumference of the can and from the top of the can to the bottom. It really does not matter if the diameter of the holes is one-quarter inch, one-half inch, or larger, so long as they will not allow the ingredients to fall through the openings.

It is beneficial to provide a vent pipe for this method, to be used in the same manner in which the vent pipe was used for the fast method. However, the diameter of the pipe for the compost can only needs to be about one and one-half inches. Either one-quarter inch holes, or one-half inch holes can be drilled completely through the pipe, and spaced about four inches apart. The length of the pipe is dependent upon the height of the can being used and whether or not a large enough hole can be drilled through the can's lid to allow the vent pipe to protrude through the lid. If drilling a hole this size is not feasible, the pipe's length will be determined by the height of the can. In this case, about a half-dozen one-quarter inch holes can be drilled into the lid, and this will allow an adequate amount of air to circulate beneath the lid and into the pipe.

Ideally, the compost can should be located as close to the house as possible since kitchen wastes can also be placed into this compost pile. There is no strenuous physical activity involved with this method of composting, and only about ten minutes are needed to turn this pile of compost on a weekly basis.

When outdoor temperatures are mild (or hot) it only takes five or six weeks to make compost by this method. Regardless of how hot the outdoor temperature is, however, the temperature of the compost pile in the compost can will not climb anywhere near the levels reached when making large quantities of compost in enclosures as described in Chapter 3. This is due to the lack of a large enough volume of organic matter within the compost can. There will not be enough heat generated to kill weed seeds, for instance, so putting weeds with seed pods attached into the compost can is discouraged. For this same reason, it is vitally important that all ingredients be shredded before being put into the container if it is desired that the compost be made as fast as possible.

It can take from thirty minutes to an hour to make a container for this compost can method (depending on the type of container and tools used) but, once the container is made, it should last a lifetime.

MAKING COMPOST IN A CAN

It is best to turn the can upside down on the moistened soil where this container will be used. The large diameter of the container will thus be resting on the surface of the soil and the small diameter (from which the bottom was removed) is now at the top. When it is time to turn the compost pile, the container can be easily lifted straight up and off the composting materials and the

Picture #34

When the compost can is lifted off the compost pile, the pile will stay in place. Position the can on the soil next to the pile, remove the vent pipe (if another one is not available for use), and place it into the can before putting the organic matter into the can. The gray vent pipe in this pile is one of the plastic tubes which golfers use in their golf bags to separate and protect their golf clubs' shafts.

organic matter will stay in place in a conically shaped pile. *(See Picture #34 above.)*

Equal amounts of green grass clippings and shredded leaves should be used when making this compost. Assuming a 32-gallon can is being used for the container, the use of similar-sized plastic trash bags to accumulate these materials is helpful in approximating (by weight) equal amounts of clippings and leaves. In other words, about a half of a bag full of fresh grass clippings and about a half of a bag full of shredded and packed leaves will be the quantities needed, and the weights of the bags will be about the same. In addition, a 5-quart pail full of soil (or about a shovel full) will be needed when combining the organic materials, along with about 4 cups of cottonseed meal or 2 cups of blood meal.

After positioning the can as mentioned above, stand the vent pipe in the center of the soil area surrounded by the can and tap it slightly into the moist soil. Begin putting the grass clippings onto the soil in the container by holding them about level with the top edge of the can and letting them scatter as they fall onto the soil. After the clippings have obtained a depth of about four inches, put about the same amount of leaves on top of the clippings by letting them also fall through the air and scatter. Stir them somewhat into the clippings with a garden fork, or reach down to them with a weed-digger and mix them in with the clippings. Sprinkle a handful of soil and a handful of fertilizer on top of the mix and then sprinkle with water. Straighten the pipe if it leaned during this activity and repeat the same sequence of adding the organic materials, soil, fertilizer and water. Pay particular attention to the moisture content of the materials because they must be damp, but not saturated. A good way to do this is to reach down into the container and scoop up a double handful of the mixed ingredients, form them into a ball, and squeeze them. If they are damp but no drops of water drip from them when they are squeezed, the moisture level is adequate. If they are too wet, sprinkle dry soil onto the mix before continuing. Continue this procedure until the pile is within an inch or two of the top of the can and then put the lid on the can. Since the can is in an upside down position, the lid will not fit tightly, or course, and a brick or some other heavy object will need to be placed on top of the lid to keep strong winds from blowing the lid off. If a large hole was drilled through the lid and the vent pipe allowed to protrude through it above the lid, a weight will still be needed to hold the lid in place unless the hole was provided in the center of the lid. It only takes about fifteen minutes to complete this method of making a compost pile in a can.

Instead of using this layering method of combining the ingredients *after* they are inside the container, they can be combined and thoroughly mixed together in a wheelbarrow before putting them into the container. This method has some advantages over the layering method in that the materials will be at a more comfortable height to work with, and they can be more thoroughly mixed together, watered, etc. When this method is used, put the materials into the can as mentioned above by scattering them and letting them fall through a couple of feet of air space as they settle into the can.

Small quantities of kitchen wastes (about enough to fill a 5-quart pail) can be mixed in with the organic materials while they are being placed into the compost can. (Large kitchen scraps such as the outer leaves of cabbage or lettuce, should be chopped or cut into small pieces, or put into a blender.) Begin putting them on top of the organic materials when the can is about one-third full, and continue adding them as the pile gets progressively higher. Finish putting them in before the pile reaches the top of the can so that about three inches of organic matter can be put on top of the kitchen wastes. If desired, similar amounts of kitchen wastes can be added to the pile after three or four days have passed, or they may be saved for a week until the pile is turned. When adding kitchen wastes to the compost pile during the middle of the week, use a hand trowel or small shovel and open a hole in the top of the organic matter, insert the kitchen wastes, and then place the materials back on top of the wastes. During the hottest part of the summer, additional water can be provided for the microorganisms in this same manner. It is helpful to also pour a few cups of water into the vent pipe so that the soil beneath the pile stays moist.

The mesophilic organisms will be the most active within the compost in the can. The mesophiles love temperatures ranging from about eighty-five degrees (Fahrenheit) to about one hundred-twenty degrees. That is the temperature range in which they experience optimum growth and the one in which they most efficiently decompose organic matter. At least, they are somewhat stereotyped in this regard. Some mesophiles are found to be at work in temperatures below this range, and some also survive and work at slightly higher temperatures. Anyway, these tiny creatures will do a good job of decomposing the compost in the can as long as they have food to eat, water to drink, and air to breathe, so to speak.

One week after the "canned compost" pile was started, the pile should be turned. Just lift the can straight up in the air, and the pile will stay put. Place the can (in the same upside down position it had been in) on the soil next to the free-standing compost pile. Remove the vent pipe from the pile and place it into the center of the can. If the soil in the can's new location is not moist, moisten it. This will let the microorganisms in this virgin soil area know that "dinner is about to be served."

Begin transferring the composting materials from the pile by getting the driest materials from the outer edges of the pile and placing them into the can. Use a small shovel, a trowel, or just use the hands to obtain these dry ingredients. (Work gloves may be worn, if desired.) Then start removing the dry materials from the top of the pile and put them into the can. After several inches of depth have been removed and placed into the can, moisten the organic matter in the container. As greater depth is reached in the old pile, moist conditions will be found. If the hands are being used, get a double handful at one time, and while holding the organic matter above the top of the can's opening, break the materials apart and let them fall into the container. If using a small shovel, the materials can be bounced up and down on the shovel and allowed to fall, or hold the shovel above the new pile with one hand and use the other hand to break apart and rake the materials from the shovel into the can. In other words, do the best possible job of aerating the organic matter. *(See Picture #35 on Page 99.)* (Usually, there will be no sign of kitchen wastes to be found.) Again, be cognizant of the amount of moisture within the pile. If moisture appears to be lacking, add water sparingly but frequently.

When the original pile is reduced to about twelve inches in height, earthworms will usually be found. (Also, when the old pile is at this height, this is the time to add chopped, cut-up, or pureed kitchen wastes to the *new* pile, but no meats or oily substances should be put in the pile.) If worms are not found at this height, they will be found a few inches lower in the pile. At least, that has been my experience.

When I first started making "canned compost" a few years ago, I chose a spot of bare soil just a few feet from the back of the garage as the location for the can. A large sycamore tree shades this area all afternoon, and the carport cover shades the area from the morning sun. If there ever was a piece of neglected soil, this was it. Nothing had ever been grown there since the house was built about fifteen

Picture #35
Use a small shovel to gather the composting ingredients from the pile and hold the shovel above the can. Then slowly rake the ingredients from the shovel with the other hand and let the organic materials be exposed to as much air as possible as they fall into the can.

years prior. About the only time that particular spot gets watered is when it rains. Needless to say, that black clay soil was as hard as concrete. Anyway, I watered the soil and then set the compost can on it and made my first pile of compost there. The first time the pile was turned, nice, big, healthy looking earthworms were found in the pile. There were only five or six large worms, but there were also a few of their offspring. So be careful when using a shovel, these *macro*organisms also do wonders for our soils, and they have built-in composting machinery in their bodies. (Those who are squeamish should wear gloves when in this area of the pile.) Gently put the earthworms into the new pile, and cover them. They will work their way down to the area of the pile in which they feel most comfortable, leaving their castings behind them.

After all of the composting ingredients have been placed into the can, put the lid on the can to keep unexpected rains from soaking the pile and leaching out the nutrients, and put an adequate weight on top of the lid. It only takes about ten minutes to turn a pile of compost made by this method. Remember to turn the pile, aerate the organic matter, and provide any needed water, every week. If no kitchen scraps are available when the pile is being turned, add a few handsful of organic fertilizer when turning the pile.

The organic matter will be decomposed, and the pile of compost will be slightly less than one half of the original volume after five or six weeks. The compost can then be used as a mulch in flower pots, hanging baskets, or other containers used for growing plants. It may also be spread on top of the soil around vegetable and ornamental plants, or it can be mixed into vacant soils in flower beds or vegetable gardens. And, naturally, it can be stored for future use, or it can be screened if a finer texture is desired. If storage facilities are not available and the compost is wanted to be aged for awhile, let the pile stand where it is and slip a plastic trash bag over the pile and weight the bag down around the bottom of the pile. Then use the can to start making another batch of compost.

This is an easy, enjoyable way to help Mother Nature decompose yard and kitchen wastes. Granted, not a large amount of compost is being made, but it can be made at the same time compost is being made by other methods. And, there is nothing wrong with having more than one compost can.

An analyst then asks, "Why not place the can right-side-up when putting the organic matter into the can? That way, it would just be a matter of tilting the can over onto its side, and flipping it over and up again."

The can could be flipped over in that manner, but the can would still have to be removed from the pile. "Turned" in this manner, the pile will only have been inverted. The ingredients which had been at the bottom of the can will now be at the top, and vice-versa. The organic matter which had been on the outside edges of the pile will still be on the outside edges, and the materials in the middle of the pile will have only been slightly disturbed. Remember, the pile must be completely taken apart in order to provide as much oxygen as possible, and to provide needed water.

In regard to having more than one compost can, homemade "compost cans" can be made of concrete reinforcing wire mesh, hog wire, or chicken wire formed into cylindrical shapes like a can. Instead of buying new trash cans, removing their bottoms, drilling holes, etc., a fifty-foot roll of any of the wire mesh materials can be purchased for about what the cost of one new trash can would cost, and the mesh could be cut into the desired lengths and formed into a half-dozen or more such enclosures. (These wire "cans" will not be made as large as the one recommended for use with the fast method in the previous chapter.) For instance, seven such enclosures can be made from a fifty-foot roll of wire mesh, and each enclosure will have a diameter of two feet. Line the inside of the enclosures with plastic bags from which the bottoms have been removed, and punch holes in the bags to admit air. Or, purchase a fifty-foot roll of the black "weed-block" plastic material used for mulching and cut it into seven equal lengths to form the lining for the cylindrical enclosures. *(See Picture #36 on Page 102.)*

Many vegetable gardeners use such homemade enclosures for caging their tomato plants, and these cages may be used during the fall and winter months to enclose either compost or leaf mold. Just place the cages on vacant garden soil and fill them with the organic matter. Every week or two during the fall and winter, remove the cages and turn the piles back into them. The psychrophilic organisms and earthworms in the garden will enjoy decomposing the organic matter during the cool (and cold) months. About a month before planting time in the spring, remove the cages, level the organic materials over the garden and till them into the soil. Spread about four pounds of cottonseed meal (or two pounds of blood meal) over each one hundred square feet of soil and then water the fertilizer into the soil to help hasten the decomposition. By planting time, the soil's microorganisms and earthworms will have turned the organic matter into humus, and the spring-planted crop will produce a bountiful harvest.

MAKING LEAF MOLD IN A CAN

Compost is the best mulching material for flower beds and vegetable gardens. Running a close second place behind compost is leaf mold. Leaf mold has almost as many nutrients as does com-

Picture #36

"Canned compost" can be made in cylindrically shaped enclosures such as those used for tomato plant cages. The "wire can" on the left has a lining made from a "weed-block" material that admits air and moisture. The one on the right is lined with a plastic trash bag that has had ventilation and drainage holes cut into it.

post, and it costs about the same to make (only a few pennies). In fact, leaf mold can also be made without adding any fertilizer, but it will take a little longer to make. However, the cool-loving psychrophiles will benefit from a "booster shot" of cottonseed meal or other fertilizer.

Leaf mold can be used for many other purposes besides mulching. It can be used in exactly the same ways compost can be used. It is ideal for use in potting soil mixes for houseplants, hanging baskets, and other containers for growing plants, and it can be tilled into the garden. The most prevalent leaves in my leaf mold are sycamore, and although they are acidic, the leaf mold tested neutral after decomposition. Leaf mold, like compost, will help neutralize the pH of soils.

Making leaf mold in a can, in a manner similar to making compost in a can, will help speed up the decomposition process. Of course, no grass clippings are used in making leaf mold. If leaf mold is wanted to be made as fast as possible, the leaves must be shredded before putting them into the container. Position the container and the vent pipe in the same manner in which they were positioned for making compost, add about four inches of shredded leaves to the can, sprinkle with soil and fertilizer, then wet the mix and stir to make sure the leaves are uniformly dampened. Then add another layer of leaves, sprinkle with soil and fertilizer, water again, and so on, until the can is full. Or the leaves can be put into a wheelbarrow and the soil, fertilizer, and water can be mixed in with them before putting the leaves into the can. Hold them above the opening in the can and let them fall and be aerated on their way into the can. When finished, place the lid on the can and weight it down. (The same amounts of soil and fertilizer that were used for making compost in a can is adequate for making leaf mold.)

Again, for the fastest decomposition, the leaf mold pile needs to be turned on a weekly basis in order to provide oxygen and moisture to the mixture. Kitchen wastes can be added at midweek, or saved until it is time to turn the pile and then incorporate them into the mix. In those areas of the country that have mild winters, leaf mold made in a can will be decomposed in about eight weeks. When temperatures reach 32° (F) and lower, the microbiological activity slows drastically, and it will naturally take longer for the leaves to decompose.

Making large quantities of leaf mold by other methods will be explained in Chapter 8.

—————— ❖ ——————

CHAPTER 5

The Tumbler Method

Using a tumbler is, by far, the easiest method of turning composting materials. The tumbler I have is quite small, so it naturally only makes small quantities of compost. But I think highly of this tumbler, and as previously mentioned, I use it at the same time in which compost is being made by other methods. As an example, it only takes about fifteen minutes to combine and place the ingredients to be composted into the tumbler, and only about one minute is needed to turn the tumbler every two or three days.

This is another method, then, that is ideal for people with limited physical abilities or for those who only have small quantities of grass clippings and leaves. But it is also for people like myself who fortunately, and gratefully, do not fit into either of those categories but want to make as much compost and leaf mold as possible. And, unlike the other methods, this compost can be turned even while it is *raining,* if need be. *(See Picture #37 on Page 105.)*

Again, if compost (or leaf mold) is desired to be made as fast as possible, all of the organic matter should be shredded or chopped into small pieces before being put into the container. This is true for the Fastest Method, the Compost Can method, the Tumbler Method or any method if speed of decomposition is important. If the speed at which organic matter is decomposed is not important, nothing needs to be shredded. All organic matter will eventually decompose. (However, from evidence I have seen recently, organic matter that is compacted, buried, compacted again and totally isolated from oxygen and water in landfill sites, might take an infinite amount of time to decompose.)

Picture #37
This small, sealed tumbler, which has a capacity of about six cubic feet, protects composting materials from rain. The umbrella protects the compos*ter* when the tumbler needs to be turned on a rainy day. (Always remove the thermometer before the first turn is begun.)

The only fault I have found with this purchased tumbler is that the ventilation holes are too large, which allows too much of the decomposed organic matter to fall out when it is being tumbled end-over-end during the last couple of weeks of the decomposition process. Cover all but one of the pre-drilled holes with scrap pieces of window screen to keep the ingredients from exiting when the tumbler is turned end-over-end. Cut the window screen into two-inch squares and use 4 self-tapping screws (one at each corner of each square) to secure the screen to the *recycled plastic* tumbler. (One of the holes is left open to allow the use of a thermometer, but be sure to remove the thermometer before tumbling the tumbler.) A rectangular-shaped plastic tub is placed beneath the tumbler to retrieve any liquified nutrients which can drip from the tumbler during periodic waterings. The plastic tub is again used to capture the compost when emptying the tumbler. After about 6 cubic feet of organic matter is decomposed in the tumbler, it yields about 2-1/2 cubic feet of compost.

During the time of year when the temperatures are mild (or hot), compost can be made in about five or six weeks in this tumbler. In the fall and winter months, leaf mold is made in about eight weeks. (Come to think of it...this could be an ideal method of making compost or leaf mold in a shed...somewhat protected from extremely cold temperatures...an umbrella would not be needed...)

The metal shaft through the center of the tumbler makes it a little awkward to combine the grass clippings and leaves if they are put into the tumbler in the "layer cake" method described in the preceding chapters. Turning the tumbler end-over-end immediately after filling it with organic materials will not actually mix the materials together either. I have found it best to mix the organic materials in a wheelbarrow before placing them into the tumbler. Use about one-half of a 32-gallon size plastic bag of grass clippings and the same amount of shredded leaves. A total of one shovel full of soil, 4 cups of cottonseed meal (or 2 cups of blood meal), and a sufficient amount of water to moisten the ingredients should be added during the mixing operation. If too much water is accidentally added to the mix in the wheelbarrow, most of the excess water can be removed from the ingredients by picking them up in both hands and squeezing and shaking the ingredients before putting them into the tumbler. Once the tumbler is full, screw the threaded lid on and place a container underneath the tumbler to catch any of the recyclable liquid nutrients which may drip from it.

My experience has been that it is best to not turn the tumbler for the first three days after filling it with organic ingredients. Allow the organic matter to heat up and begin to decompose and settle within the tumbler. There is not a great deal of heat generated within my tumbler due to the limited volume of organic matter enclosed therein. On a few occasions I have recorded readings of 140° (F), but the majority of the time the temperatures are in the 110° – 130° range, and this is a completely satisfactory temperature range for medium-fast decomposition.

After three days, stand at one side of the tumbler's stand and put one hand on the top of the tumbler and the other hand at the bottom. Then turn the tumbler from its vertical position to a horizontal position and support it in this position for a few seconds. Then complete one-half of the turn by continuing to turn the tumbler in the same direction until the tumbler is again vertical (and the top is now at the bottom), stopping again for a few seconds at this position. A definite shifting, or falling, of the ingredients within will be heard, and felt, when the tumbler reaches this upside down position. Then slowly continue the turn in the same direction until the tumbler is again "top-end-up." A definite falling of the ingredients will again be detected. After a few more seconds, repeat the turning sequence in the same slow and deliberate manner. (If the tumbler is turned too rapidly, the ingredients will not be properly aerated.) Then remove the lid and check the moisture content of the organic matter. This sealed enclosure does not lose much moisture caused by evaporation, and if the ingredients are found to be too wet, additional turnings will be needed to introduce more air after adding a few handsful of dry soil.

It is not necessary to turn the tumbler every day (unless saturated conditions are found). Otherwise, either turn it every other day, or every third day. Each day the tumbler is turned, check the moisture condition after completing the turnings. After the organic matter within the tumbler has decomposed to about one-half of the original volume, the compost is ready. Put a container below the tumbler, remove the lid and slowly turn the tumbler toward the upside down position. Before the tumbler reaches the completely upside down position some of the ingredients may begin to fall out; therefore, be ready to adjust the location of the container in which the materials will be deposited. *(See Picture #38 on Page 108.)* Another method of emptying the tumbler is to open a plastic trash bag and slip it over the tumbler's opening before beginning to turn it upside down. The bag will have to be held securely against the tumbler when turning it upside down, or some of the ingredients will fall outside the bag.

Picture #38

A six-inch-deep plastic container is positioned beneath the tumbler to collect the finished compost. This container will only hold about one cubic foot of the two and one-half cubic feet of compost produced by this tumbler.

I purchased my tumbler four or five years ago, and I do not now have the manufacturer's instructions for use or for recommendations for quantities of organic matter. However, my above prescription is just what "the patient" needs; it "cures" the compost quite rapidly every time.

Making leaf mold in the tumbler is accomplished by almost the same procedures as just described for making compost. Of course, no large amounts of grass clippings are put into the mixture when adding soil, fertilizer, and water to the shredded leaves in a wheelbarrow. (It does not hurt anything if relatively small quantities of grass clippings are picked up with the leaves when using a lawn mower to shred the leaves.) And the tumbler only needs to be turned every three or four days (or twice each week) when making leaf mold. During mild weather, leaf mold can be made in six to eight weeks in the tumbler. It usually takes several weeks longer during cold weather.

A petite housewife then asks, "Can I turn a full tumbler like you described, or will I have to get my husband to turn it?"

People who weigh close to one hundred pounds can turn a tumbler like this without straining themselves.

And then she asks, "Can kitchen wastes be used in this tumbler? You did not say anything about kitchen scraps."

Yes, kitchen scraps and wastes can be added either weekly or twice each week as long as there are no meats, bones, oils, or liquified fats in them. But again, the scraps should be chopped or cut into thumbnail size pieces or put into the blender before being added. I usually neglect to put kitchen wastes into the tumbler because I use all of them in the fast method of composting during most of the year.

A gardening friend of mine who moved here from New Jersey about five years ago has a large tumbler that holds about four times as much composting materials as what my small tumbler holds. His tumbler has a capacity of about eighteen bushels (or about twenty-two cubic feet if my arithmatic calculations are correct). Since his tumbler is located inside his garage, he is able to make compost all year. (He tells me, however, that clothespins are sometimes needed in the garage for something other than hanging clothes.) Since I have not made compost with such a large tumbler, I cannot relate any firsthand knowledge about the use of it, but my friend who likes for me to call him "Papa Joe" is well satisfied with his tumbler. *(See Picture #39 on Page 110.)*

The petite lady then asks, "Would I be able to turn that large tumbler when it is full?"

There is a possibility that slightly built persons could injure themselves trying to turn this large tumbler when it is full. I turned "Papa Joe's" tumbler on one occasion, and although I stand 5'10", and weigh 165 lbs., and am reasonably fit for most composting activities, I had to be sure my feet were solidly planted and had to use both hands to turn this full tumbler's handle. I have to admit, however, that I have never previously turned so much compost in such a short period of time.

The lady then says, "I don't think we can afford to buy one of those tumblers. Can you tell me how to make one?"

Picture #39

This shows my friend, "Papa Joe" Delbert of Garland, Texas, holding the handle of his large tumbler, which has a capacity of about twenty-two cubic feet. "Papa Joe" got tired of being retired and now works in a grocery, (which explains the source for the fifteen dozen overripe bananas used in my compost pile.) The tumbler is shown with its removable screen in place instead of the solid panel which is used for regular rotations of the container.

Although I have not yet taken the time to make a tumbler, I have visualized how such a contraption could be made. A 55-gallon drum, for instance, could be recycled for this purpose, and it could have a number of small (one-quarter inch diameter) holes drilled completely around its circumference, and in one of the ends. A "door" opening could be made into the opposite end of the drum, complete with hinges and locking mechanism. With the drum standing vertically and with the door at the top, pre-mixed organic materials could be placed into the drum. After closing and securing the door, the drum could stand in place for three days so heat could build up and decomposition could commence. The drum could then be turned onto its side on a level piece of ground and slowly rolled for a few revolutions to aerate the composting materials. Three days later, it could be slowly rolled in the opposite direction. The moisture content of the materials should be verified every third day, either before or after the drum is rolled. The dampness of the composting ingredients could be determined by obtaining some of them through the opening provided, either by reaching in with the hands, or by using a hoe to pull the ingredients toward the opening for this inspection.

One of the holes in the side of the drum, approximately in the middle of the length of the drum, should be made large enough to allow the insertion of a thermometer. When taking the compost's temperature, it would be best in this situation to just put the thermometer into the bowels of the drum for a few minutes, take the reading, and then store the thermometer elsewhere. In other words, do not go off and leave the thermometer sticking out of the drum with intentions of removing it before next rolling the drum. (When involved with such a simple activity, like rolling a drum on the ground, I can sometimes become preoccupied and most assuredly would one day find some broken glass and a mercury spill in my compost.)

This composting method would work, and I am certain that compost could be made at least as fast as with my small tumbler and probably even faster due to the larger volume of organic matter in the drum. However, instead of calling it a tumbler, this contrived device should more appropriately be named a "rolling composter." Which reminds me, always put a chucking or wedging object, such as a brick, on the ground on each side of the drum when it is lying on the ground to prevent it from rolling when unattended.

When it is time to remove the compost from the drum, a sheet of plastic or other tarp material could be placed on the ground at the end where the door is located, and a hoe or long-handled shovel could be used to obtain most of the compost. The drum could then be raised vertically above the area to let the remainder of the compost fall out the door.

Another way to make a tumbler out of a drum would be to drill a hole through each side at the middle of the drum's length to accomodate a shaft. In other words, it could be made just like the small tumbler which I have, so it could be turned end-over-end in a "ferris wheel" fashion. It would not have to be a 55-gallon steel drum either; it could be a 20- or 30-gallon plastic drum. It should not be too difficult to make a stand sturdy enough to support it.

When recycling such drums, it is important to know what they were originally used for before considering them for making compost. It may be extremely difficult, for instance, to remove certain poisonous contaminations, oils, or other petroleum products. (However, a newly developed strain of microorganisms were used in 1990, to clean up an *oil spill* off the Texas Gulf Coast. The microbes *ate* the oil and then turned it into proteins! Aren't these "little devils" amazing?)

The more I think about the composting theater...the bins...the compost cans...the tumblers...and possibly a rolling composter...a *large* shed, or a barn sure would be nice to have.

A novice vegetable gardener then offers, "I may try some of these methods you have described, but what I am most interested in is something called *green manuring*. Is that the same thing as *sheet composting?*"

The procedures involved are about the same, but the types of organic materials used are different. Green manuring refers to the growing of a green "cover crop" that is being grown specifically to be turned or tilled into the soil at a later date to add organic matter and nutrients to the soil. Sheet composting involves providing a covering of the garden area with dead (for the most part) organic materials for tilling into the soil, for the same purposes. Both of these procedures improve the structure and the nutritional value of the soil by stimulating the soil's microbial population into the production of humus.

The next chapter will explain more about these procedures.

———————— ❖ ————————

CHAPTER 6

Sheet Composting

As previously indicated a few times, I enjoy making compost. I enjoy the challenges involved in trying different methods of helping Mother Nature to decompose some of our natural resources before incorporating the organic matter into my soils. However, seldom is my compost tilled into a vegetable garden, shrub bed, or an annual flower bed, as soon as the compost is made. The huge majority of the compost is used as a mulch in those areas, and in a perennial flower bed. Only small amounts of compost are needed in hanging baskets and other containers used for growing plants. By the middle of the summer, the vegetable beds usually have an additional two-inch "insulating blanket" of compost mulch added around the plants, and any remaining compost is kept in storage for later use. At the end of the summer's growing season, the compost mulches are then tilled into the soil. Although the thickness of the compost mulch that is tilled, or turned, into the soil is more equivalent to the thickness of a couple of blankets or a quilt, rather than a thin sheet, this process is a form of *sheet* composting.

Generally, however, when vegetable gardeners or farmers speak of sheet composting, they are referring to the spreading of various other kinds of organic matter (such as leaves, grass clippings, hay, manure, etc.) over the surface of the soil, and then the tilling of that organic matter into the soil. To say it differently, the garden area is first covered with the organic matter (as a sheet is used to cover a bed), and then the area is tilled.

I know several outstanding vegetable gardeners who have never attempted to make a pile of compost (unless it was by the real slow method). They prefer to use the sheet composting method, but they do not just put a thin covering (or sheet) of organic matter

Picture #40
John Calicchio of Sunnyvale, Texas, does not have any large trees on his property, so he gets his leaves from older neighborhoods where the leaves are already bagged and are waiting to be picked up. John has 15 raised vegetable beds into which he tills approximately 75 bags of leaves every fall. He saves another 25 bags of leaves for composting in his compost bins during the following spring.

over their gardens. They put anywhere from three to six-inch-thick blanket layers of these organic materials (which are mostly leaves being recycled) on top of their gardens in the fall of the year, and then till them into their soils. *(See Picture #40 above.)* Now this thickness of materials is greater than *several* quilts *and* blankets, yet this procedure is still called *sheet* composting. And, even though I believe the terminology used for this process is a misnomer, sheet composting is one of the *best* and *easiest* ways to compost organic matter. Just let the "Big Mother" do all of her composting, right there in the soil.

Farmers were probably the first to recognize and utilize the value of another form of sheet composting, that being the tilling of plant *residues* into their large, vacant fields at the end of a growing season. (*Residue* refers to the recognizable parts of plants' remains after the plants have completed their life cycle, or are at least terminally ill.) All identifiable parts of the plants, including not only their stalks, stems, fruit, and leaves, but also their root systems, are in the residue category. Proper utilization of such crop residues is the key to soil improvement, which in turn, is the key to increased crop productivity.

It is best to let Mother Nature take her time in decomposing such raw organic materials which are incorporated into the soil so that the residues are decomposed during a period of several weeks, or even several months, depending on the availability of moisture and surrounding temperatures. In other words, the microorganisms in the soil do not *normally* need additional nitrogen to break down such *plant residues* into humus. If the speed of decomposition needs to be increased, for the planting of succeeding crops for instance, aerating the soil by additional tillings, applying supplemental nitrogen and providing adequate moisture will accomplish this objective. (Chemical forms of nitrogen fertilizer can be used most efficiently for this purpose.) The above applies to large scale farming operations as well as to backyard gardeners.

Depending on weather conditions, sheet composting can be performed during any time of the year in which vacant garden space is available. Many experienced backyard vegetable gardeners (especially city-dwellers with small back yards) use intensive gardening practices and plant successive crops as soon as the preceding plants have completed their productivity cycle and thus do no sheet composting until the end of the growing season. Others have a sufficiently large enough gardening area so that some of the garden space is allowed to be vacant during part of the growing season. For instance, a few of my raised beds are left bare during the middle of the summer so the compost mulch and other organic matter can be turned into the soil (sheet composted) during the summer. Since ambient temperatures are *hot* during the summer here in Texas, the organic matter that is thus sheet composted is completely turned into humus in a week or less. The beds that are sheet composted during the summer are then used for the fall garden's plantings, and the remaining beds are then sheet composted in late fall or early winter. People who are not

Picture #41
Sheet composting can be done at any time of the year. Grass clippings are shown being tilled into a vacant vegetable bed during August.

afforded the luxury of ample gardening space (and I have been there, also), wait until the fall or early winter to do all of their sheet composting. *(See Pictures #41 above and #42 on Page 117.)*

Gardeners who use only highly carbonaceous materials for sheet composting (such as large quantities of leaves) need to add a nitrogen supplement to the soil that is being composted. Although there are some microbes who do fairly well on a high-carbon diet, they can decompose the leaves more rapidly if they are given a "side-helping" of nitrogen. This is because leaves have very little nitrogen in relation to their carbon content, and if supplemental nitrogen is not added to the soil, the microorganisms will use the soil's available nitrogen. The largest population of soil organisms are found in those soils which have an abundant supply of organic matter that has a low carbon-to-nitrogen ratio. In other words, both carbon and nitrogen are needed for the microorganisms'

Picture #42

Ed Perna of Irving, Texas, sheet composts his garden every other fall. (In alternate years he grows cereal rye as a green manure crop in the fall.) Ed paid $25.00 for a cubic yard of commercially made compost last summer. He is going to begin making his own compost next year. Ed is a Texas Master Gardener.

energy and growth. Again, when they are provided with a somewhat "balanced diet" to their liking, along with adequate moisture and oxygen and with mild temperatures, they have a population explosion and explode into action, breaking down the organic materials into humus.

It is not possible to give a universally required amount of nitrogen fertilizer to be added for such sheet composting as just described, due to the earlier mentioned differences in soil textures, structures, climatic conditions, etc. But, for what it is worth, I use one pound of ammonium sulfate, which has a 21-0-0 analysis, for each one hundred square feet of garden area when sheet composting large amounts of shredded sycamore leaves into my alkaline soils. (For optimum speed of decomposition when sheet composting, shred the organic materials being used for this purpose, just as was prescribed for composting in above-ground enclosures.) If in doubt as to what kind of high-nitrogen fertilizer to use in your area, contact your local Extension Service. If you live in an area that has acidic soils, for instance, you should not use ammonium sulfate because it is acidic also, and would thus tend to make the soils more acidic.

Another method of recycling leaves and kitchen wastes, that is included under the umbrella of sheet composting, is more specifically called trench composting. To illustrate, let me describe how *trench* composting is done in my four-foot wide vegetable beds.

A large shovel is used to open a trench across the *width* of a bed. A trench is dug approximately eight inches deep, and the width of the trench is the same as that of the shovel being used. As each shovel full of soil is raised from the excavated area, the soil is formed into a mound along the side of the entire length of the trench. After the trench is completely dug across the width of the bed, a garden fork's tines are worked into the bottom of the trench, as deep into the soil as they will go. Then the fork's handle is first pushed in one direction, and then pulled back in the opposite direction to enlarge the holes made by the tines and to facilitate the removal of the fork. This "double-digging" use of the fork is then repeated at three more equally spaced locations within the length of the trench.

Next, shredded leaves are distributed into the trench throughout its length until the trench is full of leaves, and then they are dampened. Kitchen scraps are then distributed on top of the leaves and a handful of cottonseed meal (or about one-third of this amount of ammonium sulfate) is then sprinkled on top and watered down. *(See Picture #43 on Page 119.)* The soil that was removed and mounded adjacent to the trench is then used to cover the trenchful of organic matter; then it is formed into a slight mound and lightly tamped. If additional amounts of shredded leaves are available, another trench is then opened next to the previous one, and the same procedures are repeated. If the same gardening areas are trench composted every year, it is not necessary to use a garden fork to "double-dig" in this manner, especially not if there is no compaction such as that which can be caused by walking on the garden's soil. On the other hand, "double-digging" is a very good method to use when preparing new raised beds.

Picture #43
Trench composting is an easy way to improve soils when only limited amounts of
organic matter are available. The garden fork is at the end of a previously filled
trench. The open trench was filled with shredded leaves and kitchen scraps, sprinkled
with cottonseed meal and water, and then covered with the soil on the right. A week
later, not a trace of these materials could be found. They had already been decomposed and turned into humus.

Trench composting is an ideal method to use for recycling
leaves and kitchen wastes (and improving the soil, naturally) when
relatively small amounts of such organic matter are available at a
particular time. As more leaves become available, additional
trenches are dug. During mild weather periods of the fall, not a
trace of the organic materials can be found in a trench-composted
area after about a week. I have made such inspections with a shovel
on a number of occasions and have only been able to find what
appeared to be "moistened black gold dust" beneath the surface
of the soil. And the soil's structure is so loose and friable that the
fingers of the hand can be held straight and pressed straight down
into the soil and out of sight.

People who have small gardens do not have to use any kind of machinery, such as tillers or shredders, for any of the composting methods described in this chapter. Certainly, shredded leaves will decompose faster than whole leaves (under the same conditions), but if speed of decomposition is not critical, the leaves do not have to be shredded. Whole leaves that are incorporated into the soils when the leaves first begin falling will be decomposed by planting time in the spring if an adequate supply of nitrogen is incorporated into the soils along with the leaves.

Either a shovel or a garden fork can be used to turn leaves into the soils. People who have a number of raised vegetable beds separated by walkways, for instance, can sheet compost just one or two of the beds with a shovel on a particular day and finish the remainder of the beds in a similar fashion whenever they wish to. If they have more leaves than can be reasonably used for sheet composting in all of their beds, the leaves can be stored in plastic bags for use during the following year for composting or for the other uses described in the next two chapters.

In answer to the novice vegetable gardener's question, a *green manure* crop (or cover crop) is grown for the specific purpose of being *recycled* into the soil in which it is grown. Although it is difficult to imagine how or why such a crop would ever be sent to a landfill site, I will explain why a green manure crop is valuable to a beginning gardener's soils.

There are many different crops which can be grown for green manuring. For example, alfalfa or any of the clovers, barley, buckwheat, any of the legumes, oats, ryes and winter vetch can be grown for green manuring. Some of these crops perform better than some of the others in different parts of our country, and they are best planted at different times of the year due to climatic reasons. The best advice I can give in regard to which crops to plant for green manures (and please forgive this repetitive guidance) is for you to contact your local Extension Service and find out which crops are recommended for your geographical location.

However, I *can* provide a testimonial in regard to the use of an outstanding green manure crop with which I have had experience. The crop is commonly called cereal rye (Elbon rye) and is planted anytime from the middle of August to the middle of September in my area. The seed is about the size of wild rice, and it is easy to broadcast over a pre-fertilized and dampened soil. The planting area's soil should be loosened with a rake or other convenient tool prior to broadcasting the seed. Then lightly rake the seeds into the soil, tamp, and then spray with water. Moisten the soil every other day until the seeds germinate, which usually takes between 7 and 10 days. I have found that birds love the cereal rye seeds, and after they dine on all of the seeds that are not completely covered, they will scratch into the soil to acquire what is evidently a delectable meal for them. This is not too much of a problem in my four-foot wide planting beds, however, because I sometimes roll out a length of chicken wire over the bed, which deters the birds from harvesting the seeds. (The chicken wire is also used at times to prevent an itinerate alley cat from scratching and messing around in newly seeded beds.) I broadcast two pounds of the seeds in a one hundred square foot bed and always get a good stand, even without the chicken wire (if I throw a few handsful of the seeds in an adjacent area for the birds).

Within a few weeks after germination, the cereal rye is about five or six inches tall, and it is then mowed. The clippings are left in the beds to decompose, naturally. Several weeks later the rye will again require mowing. A few times, I neglected mowing when I should have done so, and the rye grew to between 8 and 10 inches tall. I then made several passes over the crop with a weed-eater, reducing the height of the plants a little each time. About the middle of January, I begin turning the rye over, literally, by sticking a shovel beneath a clump and then turning it upside down. The sharp point of the shovel is used to slice or chop through the clump's roots to hasten decomposition. After the entire crop is turned over (green side down), it is not disturbed for about a week. At that time, it is tilled and again allowed to decompose for another week. Then I till it again.

This may seem to be a lot of work, but it really is not in this size of a planting. Anyway, I believe it is well worth the effort, and I heartily recommend it to gardeners in my part of our country. One of the side benefits of this crop is that research has shown that cereal rye's root systems trap root knot nematodes during certain stages of their growth. (Root knot nematodes are microscopic organisms, but they are *not* the beneficial kind.) These nematodes cause knots, or swellings, in the roots of susceptible plants and can severely damage certain vegetable and fruit crops. In addition, the numerous mowings provide clippings which decompose, and the turning under and tilling of the crop adds plenty of additional organic matter to the soil. The humus derived from the decomposition of the cereal rye is rich in nitrogen and other nutrients in a form which makes the nutrients readily available for successive plantings. So a *green* cover crop, turned into and decomposed in the soil, produces a *fertilized* soil and is consequently called *green manure*.

A senior citizen who is evidently more than just a few years my senior then says, "A number of years ago, I could have used all of the methods of composting you have been describing, but now I just don't feel up to any of them. Tell me how I can stop sending my grass clippings and leaves to the landfill without doing all that work."

The next chapter describes the "slow" and "not so slow" methods which are in the "no work" and "little work" categories, respectively.

❖

CHAPTER 7

The Slow and Not-So-Slow Methods

For those people who are physically unable, do not have the time, or just do not want to make compost by any of the fast or medium fast methods described in the preceding chapters, there are a few more methods of making compost which involve little or no work. These methods are also adaptable for those who have ample supplies of yard wastes as well as for those who have little such wastes.

Naturally, the methods of composting that require *no work* are also the methods which take the longest amount of time for the organic materials to decompose. Organic matter such as leaves, grass clippings, shrub prunings and kitchen wastes can all be put into a pile on top of the soil, and they will eventually be decomposed by the soil's microorganisms and earthworms. No fertilizer and no water *have* to be added to the pile, and the pile can be either exposed to the elements, or a plastic or canvas tarpaulin can be used to cover it. Such a pile can assume whatever dimensions are practicable for the person who is using this method and the pile does not have to be completely built in one day. As additional organic materials become available, they can be added to the pile at any time. The additional grass clippings, weeds, leaves, dead flower stalks or other plant residues can all be put on the top, or on the sides of the pile. A pile made in this manner will not generate enough heat to sterilize the materials used, nor kill any weed seeds, so use good judgment in using such suspected ingredients. When additional kitchen wastes become available, they too may be added to the pile although this can best be done by opening a hole in the pile to receive the garbage and then covering it up, rather than just putting such wastes on top of the pile.

Quite a few years ago, I had an uncle who was highly skilled in making compost by using this no-work method, and this was the only method he used on his small lot in the city. The compost pile was circular shaped with a diameter of about ten feet at the base of the mounded ingredients, and the pile was kept covered with a couple of canvas tarpaulins. I am not sure how long the pile had been in existence when I first saw it, but I remember exactly how my uncle made use of it.

Beginning in a clockwise direction, he would remove compost from the "12 o'clock" location of the pile in late spring, or early summer. Then, when grass clippings and other organic materials were available, they were put into the area from which the compost had been removed. A few weeks later, he removed compost from the "3 o'clock" area of the pile and then he began backfilling that area with raw organic matter. When the "3 o'clock" location was again filled with organic materials, compost was then removed from the "6 o'clock" spot in the pile, and so on, "around the clock." By the end of the summer, the organic materials which had been put into the "12 o'clock" location of the pile at the beginning of the summer were only partially decomposed, but compost was not needed nor was a spot needed for grass clippings. Kitchen wastes were put into the pile whenever they were available. When the falling leaves accumulated in large enough amounts, one side of the tarp was folded back, the leaves were put onto the pile and moistened and then covered with the tarp. The pile was never turned, and there was no vent pipe. Yet there were no objectionable odors coming from this anaerobically decomposed pile.

Kitchen scraps and garbage were continually inserted into the pile as they were available during the remainder of the year and through the following spring in the same chronological sequence. However, none were put into the "12 o'clock" location during the spring because that was the spot from which finished compost would be first removed the following summer. Uncle Ben knew how to make "no work" compost.

As previously stated, "no work" compost piles can be any shape or any size. There is, of course, nothing wrong with putting such a pile in an enclosure of some sort, if one is available, to help make the sides of the pile more vertical and thus have more depth. If some kind of a vent pipe is also available, use it to form an air shaft in the center of the pile when the pile is being built. If a vent pipe is not handy, stand a 2" by 4" piece of lumber in the center of the area where the pile is to be established, and after the pile has reached the desired height, the 2" by 4" lumber can be removed, leaving a natural air shaft opening in the pile. This opening will then provide a vertical trough to allow the admittance of water to the middle and to the bottom of the pile. Although the pile does not have to be covered in order for it to be decomposed, a covering for the pile will prevent many of the natural nutrients from being leached or washed out of the pile by heavy rains. While the organic materials are being placed into a pile, add a little fertilizer every now and then and water it down. Just this much effort will help speed the decomposition even if the pile is never turned and aerated.

During this past summer, "Papa Joe" took me to an apartment complex about a mile from his home to show me how some of the apartments' tenants utilized the slow method of composting. There is a large vacant area (an acre or two, at least) next to the apartments, and a couple living in one of the apartments had cleared off an area for a vegetable garden. They have had great success in growing their fresh vegetables there. The couple obtain grass clippings from the people who mow the grass and do other landscaping around the apartments, such as trimming the shrubs, planting flowers, etc. The shrub prunings, spent flowers, grass clippings, vegetable plant residues and even a few weeds are put into a pile to be decomposed by Mother Nature. The couple has been gardening here for several years, and each year they pile all of the organic materials at one end of the pile and begin removing compost from the other end of the pile. *(See Picture #44 on Page 126.)*

Across the alley from the apartment complex are some single-family residences, and a few of the homeowners have started donating their yard wastes to the gardeners' compost pile. One of the homeowners who does not have enough room in her yard for a garden, now gardens in another spot in the vacant field and has built the same kind of a compost pile right next to her garden. At the edge of a vegetable garden is an ideal location for the pile. *(See Picture #45 on Page 127.)*

However, when composting organic matter is piled in an open area and is unprotected from rains, a fertilizer that is high in its nitrogen percentage needs to be added to the soil into which the organic matter is to be put. During the long period of time that

Picture #44

Grass clippings, leaves and plant residues are put into a large pile to be decomposed by Mother Nature in this vacant field next to an apartment complex in Garland, Texas. The compost is used by a couple who cleared an area of this vacant land for their vegetable garden.

the pile is being decomposed, the microorganisms will use up whatever amount of nitrogen is in the pile (and not washed out by rainfall). If such nitrogen depleted organic matter is put into the soil without a nitrogen fertilizer being used as a supplement, the soil's microbial population will use whatever nitrogen is available in the soil in their attempt to decompose the organic matter into humus, and the soil will then have a nitrogen deficiency.

There are no rules that govern the amount of work or the amount of time that is required for any of the composting methods, whether they be in the fast category or the slow category. The guidelines for making compost as fast as possible, for instance, can be altered to fit the individual composter's needs, and there are, of course, many other slow methods of composting than what has thus far been explained. It is this flexibility aspect which makes the art of composting so universally appealing, along with the knowl-

Picture #45
This shows the slow method of composting at the edge of a vegetable garden.
(This is an ideal location for a compost pile.)

edge that Mother Nature is very adaptable to our innovative modifications. Therefore, there are many such modified composting methods which are in the middle of the speed range between the very fast and the very slow methods. These, then, are the methods which I refer to as "not so slow" which could also be called "not so fast" or "little work" methods.

One of my favorite "happy medium" methods of composting involves the building of a pile in an enclosure and constructing the pile in a layered manner as described in Chapter 3, utilizing the basic principles of the fast method. Begin by standing the vent pipe in the center of the enclosure as before and alternately pile grass clippings and moistened shredded leaves with kitchen wastes, fertilizer, and soil being added periodically. When the pile is three feet tall (or higher, if possible), spread two shovels full of soil or leftover compost over the top of the pile and moisten. Then cover the top of the pile with a sheet of plastic or several plastic trash bags and weight them down. Admittedly, there is as much work involved in building this pile as there is in establishing a pile for the fast method, but no more work has to be done to this pile. All of the pile will be sufficiently decomposed, with the possible exception of the thin outer side layers, in about eight months.

If a pile is built in this same manner, turned at monthly intervals and provided with adequate moisture, it will be decomposed after about five months. Or if the pile is turned every two weeks and is properly moistened during the turning process, it will be ready in about three months. The indefinite estimates of the amount of time for these piles to be decomposed is due to the uncertainty of climatic conditions and the time of the year when the piles are first constructed. Again, the frequency at which such piles are turned and the attentiveness of the person turning the pile can either speed up or delay the decomposition process.

What I have described in this chapter are the slow methods of making compost which I have either had successful experiences with, or successful methods which I have observed others (such as my uncle) have had. There are many other methods for turning yard wastes and kitchen wastes into compost which I have not yet experienced or observed, such as composting in pits dug into the ground or making enclosures for earthworm composting, etc. (Both of those methods are interesting to me, and I plan to try them in the not too distant future.) There should be no difficulty in finding books on these other methods of composting in libraries or for sale at book stores.

The senior citizen then says, "I can probably make compost the way your uncle did, but I do not have a tarpaulin or even enough room for a pile that big. Isn't there some other way I can use my grass clippings and leaves and not do so much work?"

Grass clippings and leaves do not have to be bagged and carried to a composting enclosure or piled up in the yard somewhere. (But they certainly should not be put by the trash to be carried to the landfill.) The next chapter will explain how these natural resources can benefit your lawn and shrub beds and save you time, money, and effort.

———————— ❖ ————————

CHAPTER 8

Other Uses For
Kitchen and Lawn Wastes

As mentioned in Chapter 3, I do not normally collect and bag the grass clippings when mowing my bermuda grass lawn. The grass clippings are only bagged on those occasions when the grass is allowed to grow a little taller than normal before it is cut (such as, when grass clippings are needed for a compost pile). As a general rule, the grass clippings are allowed to remain in the lawn where they are decomposed by Mother Nature. By not bagging the grass clippings, no trash bags need to be purchased, about thirty percent less time is required to mow the lawn, and nothing is sent to the landfill. According to the Texas Agricultural Extension Service, allowing the grass clippings to decompose in the lawn provides enough nutrients to the lawn that the amount of fertilizer required is reduced by approximately twenty-five percent. (Grass clippings contain nitrogen, phosphorus, potassium and some of all of the trace elements needed by plants.) The decomposition of the grass clippings in the soil naturally provides additional organic matter which increases microbial activity and the resultant increase in humus which, in turn, improves the retention of moisture in the soil and thus a reduction in the amount of water which homeowners need to apply to their lawns. (This is *recycling* in a manner surpassing all others!)

Dr. Bill Knoop, Extension Turfgrass Specialist, The Texas A&M University System, and author of *The Complete Guide To Texas Lawn Care*, has been instrumental in promoting the "Don't Bag It" and "Let It Be" programs in the State of Texas. As of January 1991, over 100 cities have adopted these "waste-saver lawn care plans" which recommend leaving grass clippings on the lawn.

In order to derive all of the benefits from not bagging grass clippings as described in the preceding paragraph, attention must be given to the proper amount and frequency of *fertilizing*, the proper amount and frequency of *watering*, and the proper amount of the grass's leaf area that is removed when the lawn is mowed (which is accomplished by the proper frequency of *mowing*).

FERTILIZING*
It is recommended that bermuda grass lawns in my county be nourished with fertilizers having either a 3-1-2 NPK ratio, or a 4-1-2 NPK ratio (such as 15-5-10, or 16-4-8) and that at least one-half of the nitrogen in the fertilizer be in a slow release or slowly soluble form. Such lawns are fertilized four times during the growing season at six-week intervals with the first application being made about the middle of April. By leaving the grass clippings on the lawn and thus obtaining the natural nutrients which the clippings provide, only one pound of nitrogen is recommended to be applied per one thousand square feet. For example, since there are 6 pounds of nitrogen in a forty-pound bag of 15-5-10 fertilizer (15% of 40 = 6), such a bag provides the recommended amount of nitrogen for a six thousand square foot area. If the grass clippings are not left on the lawn, the same bag of fertilizer can only furnish the nitrogen needed for a lawn of approximately forty-five hundred square feet.

WATERING*
Warm season grasses need the equivalent of a one-inch rain every week during hot, dry weather. Of course, if there is no rain, the homeowner must supply the needed amount of water. In this respect, a rain gauge will pay for itself during the same year in which it is purchased if it is used properly. Empty the gauge at the end of the day on which rain is received and record the amount of rainfall on a calendar. If an automatic water sprinkling system is calibrated to turn on during a week following an adequate amount of rainfall, turn the system off. Then, if no rain is recorded after a week has passed, turn the sprinkler system on again. (It is best to wait until the soil begins to dry out and then provide the total amount of water needed, all in one day.) Frequent sprinklings several times a week do more harm than good because this prac-

tice encourages shallow root development. Watering the lawn early in the morning, instead of during the middle of the day, is more efficient since less water is lost to evaporation. Watering the lawn late in the evening, as the sun is setting, maximizes the activity of disease-causing bacteria.

MOWING*

Lawn grasses should be mowed frequently enough so that no more than one-third of the leaf surface is removed at any one time. As an example, if a grass is desired to be cut to a height of two inches, it should be mowed when it is no more than three inches tall. I follow the rate and frequency of fertilizing and watering that is recommended for my grass and soil and average mowing the lawn every five days. Let me give a comparison between the amount of time required to mow a lawn and bag the clippings and the amount of time that is needed to mow the same lawn and leave the clippings where they fall. To simplify the comparison, assume it takes one hour to mow a particular lawn and to bag the grass clippings. If that lawn is maintained in that fashion for thirteen weeks and it is only mowed on a weekly basis, then a total of thirteen hours will be consumed by that operation. If that same lawn is mowed every *five* days and the clippings are left on the lawn during a thirteen week period, the lawn will be mowed eighteen times. However, by saving approximately thirty percent of the time required for each mowing (by not bagging the clippings), less total time will be expended even though the lawn is mowed five additional times during the thirteen week period. (And, in addition to all of the previously mentioned benefits, it is so much easier than mowing a lawn and bagging the clippings on a weekly basis.)

So, those people who can not, or do not want to make compost out of their grass clippings can stop sending their clippings to the landfill by letting the clippings be decomposed in their lawns. They will save money by not having to buy as many trash bags, by not buying as much fertilizer and by not using as much water on their lawns. If they occasionally let the grass get too tall between mowings, they can bag the clippings and then take the bag over to

* *The recommended rates and frequencies for fertilizing, watering, and mowing of your lawn in your location can be obtained from your Extension Service.*

a shrub bed and spread the clippings in a thin layer around the shrubs. If the layer of grass clippings used in this manner (as a mulch) is over an inch in depth, the clippings may become matted and prevent light rains or waterings from penetrating the clippings properly. After about a week has passed, depending on weather conditions, the grass clippings will have lost their green color and become dried, and they can then be lightly stirred with a rake to loosen them. Later, if more clippings are desired to be put on top of the existing layer, moisten the existing layer before applying the additional clippings. Or, shredded leaves, or hay or straw, or chopped hedge trimmings can be mixed with the grass clipping mulch to prevent the clippings from matting.

The senior citizen then says, "I thought leaving grass clippings on a lawn the way you described would cause a thatch problem."

Thatch problems in lawns are caused by excessive amounts of nitrogen fertilizers, excessive amounts of water, and by excessive amounts of pesticides. Too much nitrogen fertilizer stimulates rapid growth and will cause more frequent mowings of the grass and thus excessive amounts of clippings to be decomposed. Excessive amounts of water reduce the availability of oxygen in the soil, thus reducing the population of the aerobic microorganisms. Excessive pesticide usage kills a large percentage of these same organisms which are needed to decompose the grass clippings. In other words, if the quantity of grass clippings is greater than that which can be decomposed by the soil's microorganisms, the lawn can develop a thatch problem. Follow the recommendations of your Extension Service in regard to fertilizing, watering, and mowing your lawn grass and there will be no thatch problem.

And lastly, the senior citizen says, "Okay. I believe I can handle my grass clippings. But what am I to do with all of these leaves in order to keep from sending them to the landfill?"

Leaves are another good source of natural nutrients which can be used in many ways other than for composting and for making leaf mold. Leaves contain nitrogen, phosphorous, potassium and several other nutrients which are needed by growing plants. Unlike grass clippings, however, leaves have a high carbon-to-nitrogen ratio, and the soil's microorganisms will need a nitrogen source to help them to break down this carbonaceous matter. If large quantities of leaves are used as a mulch for flower beds, vegetable gardens or other areas to cover bare soil around growing plants, the microorganisms will use whatever nitrogen is available for their enzymic activities. If supplemental nitrogen is not provided by fertilizers or nitrogenous plant residues, the microbial activities can cause a nitrogen deficiency which will adversely effect plants which are growing in the immediate area.

Excessive quantities of leaves in the fall can be stored for use during the following spring and summer. They may be stored in any kind of enclosure including plastic trash bags, or the leaves can just be placed into a pile. Shredding the leaves by using a lawn mower, blower-vac, or a weed-eater as described in earlier chapters will greatly reduce their volume and thereby lessen the amount of storage space required.

When green grass clippings become available in the following year, the leaves that were saved during the winter can be mixed with the clippings and used as a mulch. Just spread a thin layer of the clippings over the area to be mulched, then a layer of leaves, then more clippings, and so on until the mulch is about four inches in depth. Since green grass clippings are high in nitrogen, no nitrogen fertilizer needs to be added to the mulch if the quantities of clippings and leaves used are about equal. A mulch composed of green grass clippings and shredded leaves will readily allow water and air to reach the surface of the soil beneath the mulch. Additional quantities of fresh clippings and leaves can be added as the mulch settles and begins to decompose.

If sufficient quantities of fresh grass clippings are not available, leaves can be used as a mulch by themselves. However, it is best not to use whole leaves as a mulch, especially if the mulch is to be more than two inches thick, since whole leaves tend to become matted almost as badly as do thick mulches made of grass clippings. Shredded leaves can be applied as a mulch with a depth up to six inches but always apply a fertilizer with a high nitrogen percentage to the soil and water it well before applying the leaves, for the reason previously mentioned. And lastly, leaves can be worked into any vacant area of soil (along with some nitrogen fertilizer) to help improve the humic content of the soil.

Those people who are physically able and have the desire to make large quantities of leaf mold can do so during the fall, winter and spring. Some people use tall (4- or 5-feet) cylindrical en-

Picture #46

Warren Frazier of Dallas, Texas, makes leaf mold in these 4' by 4' by 3' enclosures every fall. He uses the enclosure on the left and the one in the middle to turn the leaf mold about once each month during the fall and winter. The plant residues in the enclosure at the right will be added to this coming fall's crop of leaves. Warren is a Texas Master Gardener.

closures made of wire for this purpose. Others use enclosures made of concrete blocks or bricks or even plywood. Those who have composting bins use the bins for making leaf mold during the time of the year when composting activities cease. Some even use the space between their fence and the alley at the back of their property. *(See Pictures #46 above and #47 on Page 135.)*

Enclosures for making leaf mold do not have to be tall since there is no heat generated by the decomposition of leaves even approaching that which is generated during the composting of leaves mixed with grass clippings. The leaves do not have to be shredded, nor do they have to be aerated or turned.

About ten years ago I met a lady who made leaf mold in her back yard in an area that was about five feet wide and thirty feet

Picture #47

Leaf mold, or compost enclosures can be made of various materials, in any size desired, and they can be put in unusual (and unused) locations.

long. All she used to enclose the area were concrete blocks that were eight inches tall and sixteen inches long. The leaves were just spread evenly over the area, fertilized and moistened initially, and left alone to be decomposed naturally. When more leaves became available, she spread a thin layer of soil and a sprinkling of fertilizer over the existing layer of leaves and moistened them before adding the next layer of leaves. By the time the trees were bare of leaves, she had a sloping mound of leaves that was, at the most, two feet high in the middle of the enclosure. The following year she merely shoveled the upper layer of leaves out of the way and then started filling her wheelbarrow with the prettiest leaf mold ever seen.

The senior citizen then says, "I just thought of another question. Can kitchen scraps and garbage be put into those piles of leaves?"

It is best not to put kitchen wastes into uncovered piles of leaves that are not in enclosures because scavenging varmints can be attracted by the smell of the foodstuffs. (And some municipalities still have laws against such disposal of kitchen wastes.)

However, for those people who do not use their grass clippings and leaves for composting, there are some other ways to dispose of kitchen wastes besides sending them to the landfill. There are many knowledgeable gardeners who bury their kitchen wastes (again, no meats or fats) in their gardens. They just dig out a couple of shovels full of soil, deposit the kitchen wastes into the hole and then cover the wastes with the soil. The soil's microorganisms decompose these wastes and turn them into humus. During warm weather, such wastes are totally decomposed and literally cannot be identified a week later when digging in the spot in which they were deposited. *(See Picture #48 on Page 137.)*

I purchased a 32-gallon *recycled plastic* trash can over a year ago and have been using it as an outdoor kitchen waste disposal "off and on" since that time. The reason for the "off and on" reference is that most of the year such kitchen wastes are used in compost piles and leaf mold enclosures, and occasionally my wife puts the kitchen wastes into the kitchen sink's electric garbage disposal. To prepare the trash can for kitchen waste disposal, sixty one-half-inch diameter holes were drilled into the bottom of the can and about thirty such holes were drilled around the side of the container, about two or three inches from its bottom. A one-foot deep hole, conforming to the diameter of the can's bottom, was dug into the ground just outside our garage's door. This "outdoor garbage disposal unit" was then placed into the hole in the ground, and the soil was then packed around it. At the current rate of use, this plastic can may not need to be emptied for several more years. The soil's microorganisms and macroorganisms turn the kitchen wastes into humus almost as fast as such wastes are presently being put into the can. Each time kitchen wastes are put into the can, a sprinkling of dry soil is put on top of the wastes. The lid of the can fits snugly, there is no odor, and there are no scavenging varmints which can enter through the one-half-inch diameter holes at the bottom of the can, at least not in my part of the country. *(See Picture #49 on Page 138.)*

I only know of one such manufactured device that can be used

Picture #48

Kitchen scraps can be buried in vacant garden areas at any time of the year. The soil's microorganisms will quickly decompose such wastes during warm weather. The buried location can be covered with boards, chicken wire, hog wire, etc., to prevent pets or stray animals from digging in the area before the wastes have been decomposed.

primarily for outdoor disposal of garbage. It is called "The Green Cone™ Composter," and it is available from Solarcone, Inc., P.O. Box 67, Seward, Illinois 61077-0067. The 1991 price of this unit is $90.00 plus shipping, handling, and appropriate taxes. In addition to being used for composting garbage, the Green Cone™ can also compost small quantities of yard wastes. There are many sources

Picture #49
A total of about ninety holes were drilled into the bottom, and within a few inches of the bottom of this "industrially recycled plastic" garbage can. The can is buried twelve inches into the soil at a convenient location for kitchen waste disposal.

for readymade above-ground composting enclosures, tumblers, leaf-eaters, chipper/shredders and other gardening and recycling equipment. Many of these are available from department and hardware stores and from such mail order sources as Burpee Seed Co., Warminster, PA, 18974, Parks Seed Co., Greenwood, SC 29647, Porter & Son, Seedsmen, Stephenville, TX 76401, Gardener's Supply, Burlington VT 05401, and The Plow & Hearth, Orange, VA 22960.

There is really no excuse then for homeowners to not recycle their kitchen and yard wastes. Composting enclosures can be made easily and inexpensively, or they can be purchased in prices ranging from about $50.00 and up. Those people who are energetic can make large quantities of compost in relatively short periods of time while others can make compost at their leisure. If yard wastes are not to be composted, they can be used as an organic mulch, or for making leaf mold.

Such utilization of these natural resources should not be thought of as waste disposal methods. Instead, they are methods by which we can make so many improvements to our soils, plants, and to our environment as a whole, and they cost us nothing. Nor should our nations' landfill problem be thought of as just an *opportunity* for our generation. It is our ongoing *responsibility* to solve this troublesome and embarrassing situation for the benefit of future generations.

According to an EPA document entitled, "This Compost Went to Market," in the not too distant future we may not have a choice to make in regard to what we do with our yard wastes. This document states, "between now and January 1, 1993, at least eight more states (Connecticut, Florida, Iowa, Minnesota, North Carolina, Ohio, Pennsylvania, and Wisconsin) will join Illinois and New Jersey in officially banning some or all types of their yard trimmings from landfill disposal (Glenn, 1989)."

❖

CHAPTER 9

Let's Get Involved!

The United States' current rate of 160 million tons of wastes that are sent to landfills each year could fill a convoy of 10-ton garbage trucks 145,000 miles long — long enough to circle the equator almost six times. And as a nation, we are producing an ever-increasing amount of municipal trash. According to the Environmental Protection Agency, in every year since 1960 our country has experienced a rise in both the total tons of wastes generated and the total pounds of wastes per person. Referred to as the "throwaway society," we produce almost twice as much solid waste as other developed countries.

A prime example of the difficulty which communities have experienced in disposing of garbage is the ill-fated journey of the garbage barge, Mobro. The Mobro traveled on a six-month odyssey of over 6,000 miles, including six states and three countries, before it found a home — in New York, where it came from!

All levels of our society have underestimated the significance of proper municipal solid waste management. Local, state, and federal governments have all underestimated the importance of providing safe and effective waste management. Industry has designed, manufactured, and packaged products with little regard to how they will eventually be disposed. Individuals consume products and generate wastes (approximately 3.6 pounds per person per day) with little thought of disposal issues. And, disposal facility owners and operators have historically considered environmental issues to be of secondary concern. *(See Figure 1 on Page 141.)*

As a nation, we currently recycle approximately 10% of our wastes and incinerate only another 10%. The remaining 80% of our municipal waste is disposed of in landfills, and landfill sites are

ANNUAL PERCENT OF TOTAL WASTES SENT TO LANDFILLS

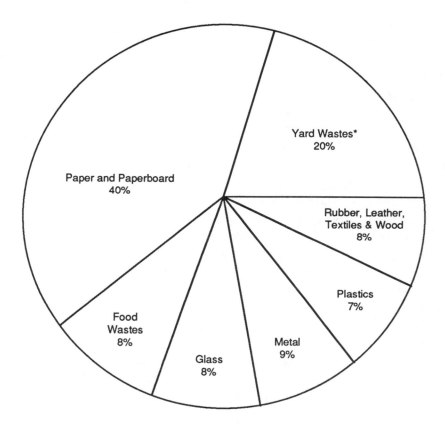

Figure 1

- Every Sunday more than 500,000 trees are used to produce the 88% of newspapers that are never recycled.

- We throw away enough glass bottles and jars to fill the 1,350-foot twin towers of New York's World Trade Center every two weeks.

- American consumers and industry throw away enough aluminum to rebuild our entire commercial airfleet every three months.

- We throw away enough iron and steel to continuously supply the needs of all of our nation's automakers.

During the summer and fall, yard wastes account for 50% or more of the total discarded materials that are sent to landfill sites.

rapidly being filled and closed all across our country. It has been estimated that more than 2400 of the present 6000 landfill sites will be full by 1995.

Incinerators are not able to safely handle the volume of trash that is produced. The seasonal nature of grass clippings and leaves, for instance, can cause incinerators designed to handle this type of solid waste to be over-sized and operate inefficiently. The high moisture content of these yard wastes inhibits complete combustion and results in the availability of little net usuable energy for power generation (in waste-to-energy facilities), and such burning contributes to carbon dioxide and nitrogen oxide emissions. Aside from the technical problems associated with the *incinerating* of yard wastes, sending them to *landfills* is an unnecessary, inefficient, and wasteful disposal of these natural resources which we can recycle and utilize in our own back yards.

In the Introduction, I referred to the EPA's study, *Yard Waste Composting — A Study of Eight Programs,* which was completed in April 1989. The conclusion of this study showed that the percentage of yard wastes diverted from landfill sites is highly dependent on community and household *participation* levels, the composition of the yard waste stream and the types of yard wastes composted or shredded. And, that the number of processing steps, including technologies used, shredding, screening, monitoring, testing, etc., is related to the available land, labor and capital and the desired *quality* and *value* of the end product.

Although there are approximately nine hundred centralized yard waste composting facilities operated by municipalities or private companies in the United States, none of them can make the high quality, uncontaminated compost which you and I, individually, can make. In addition, by leaving our grass clippings on our lawns or using them along with our leaves to make compost or mulch, we are eliminating the costs of collecting, transporting and processing which would otherwise be paid for by our communities.

My main purpose for writing this book is to get as many people as possible to begin using their yard wastes and kitchen wastes to make compost and leaf mold, to leave their grass clippings on their lawns, or to use yard wastes as mulches and thereby stop sending these valuable resources to landfills. Although there are many gardening books that explain what compost is, how it improves soils and how it can be made, most of the books seem to have been written mainly for those who are involved in vegetable gardening. I hope I have convinced you that you do not have to be a vegetable gardener to make good use of compost and other organic matter in your flower and shrub beds.

However, as illustrated in *Figure 1,* there are a number of other items which we citizens need to recycle in order to conserve land-fill space, to save virgin materials, and to save energy.

PAPER

Paper products, mainly newspapers and cardboard, account for 40% of the total volume of wastes sent to landfills each year. It has been estimated that recycling a stack of newspapers only four feet high can save one tree, and it only takes about half as much energy to turn recycled paper into reuseable paper as compared with making new paper products from trees. The prices paid for old newspapers by recycling centers varies in different communities, and the prices fluctuate based on the recyclers' ability to sell the paper to paper mills. Prices paid for old newspapers in my area, for instance, have ranged from one cent per pound to one cent for four pounds, and there are times when recycling centers will only accept the newspapers and pay nothing for them. As more and more of the old paper mills are renovated and modified to be able to recycle newspapers and other paper products, and as more new de-inking plants are built to handle the large volumes of old newsprint, more stable prices can be expected. However, whether we receive a dollar for every one hundred pounds of paper we collect or whether we receive nothing at all, we should discontinue sending paper products to take up space in our landfills, causing more trees to be cut down, and wasting energy. Saving daily news-papers costs us nothing, nor is it time consuming. *(See Picture #50 on Page 144.)*

Corrugated cardboard boxes (the type of cardboard that has a ribbed layer between two flat layers) are easy to break open so that they lie flat in storage. When enough have been accumulated, they should be bundled so they can be more easily carried. The price paid for corrugated cardboard does not fluctuate like the newspa-per prices and generally runs about one cent per pound.

Colored ledger paper, high quality non-glossy white paper and

Picture #50

A cardboard box can be made into an ideal container for accumulating daily newspapers. Cut a "V"-shaped notch at the top of each side and at each end as shown, and put two pieces of twine long enough to lie across the bottom and to come up over the sides and ends. When the container is full of old newspapers, tie the twine from side-to-side and from end-to-end and then lift the newspapers from the container. Every fourth time the container is filled (with newspapers approximately one-foot high), enough newspapers can be recycled to save a tree. Old newspapers should be kept either inside the house or in the garage. They cannot be recycled if they are allowed to get wet.

computer print-out paper can be sold to recycling centers, and their prices run from about three and one-half cents per pound to about seven and one-half cents per pound, respectively.

ALUMINUM

Aluminum cans are easy to accumulate for recycling. They should be rinsed with water and flattened so they do not take up so much space in storage containers. Approximately twenty-eight aluminum soft drink cans weigh one pound, and each pound currently sells

---

for about thirty-five cents in my area. New aluminum products can be made from recycled aluminum using only about 5% of the amount of energy required to make aluminum from ore.

GLASS
Glass bottles and jars are presently selling for two cents per pound. They should be rinsed, and lids and caps removed before taking them to the recycling center. Some recyclers will not accept mixed colors of glass products and require that they be separated by the three main colors: brown, clear, and green. Making new products from recycled glass saves about one-third of the energy required to make glass from raw materials.

PLASTIC
Plastic containers are also presently being bought for two cents per pound. The most commonly recycled plastics are two-liter soft drink bottles, milk jugs, and shampoo, liquid dishwashing, and fabric-softener containers. Approximately 60% less energy is used to make new plastic items from recycled plastics. Some recyclers request that homeowners separate the high-density polyethylene (HDPE) plastics (such as milk jugs, shampoo and detergent containers) from the polyethylene teraphthalate (PET) plastic which is the plastic used to make two-liter soft drink bottles.

OTHER RECYCLABLES
In addition to aluminum drink cans, there are many other aluminum products which homeowners can recycle. These include frozen food containers, foil food wraps, pie plates, pots and pans and larger items such as storm windows and doors, lawn furniture, appliances, aluminum siding, etc. Many such items are also made of steel, and if in doubt as to whether the metal is aluminum or steel, an inexpensive magnet can be used to make this determination. (If the item is made of aluminum, the magnet will not adhere to it.) Most recycling centers which accept aluminum will also accept steel, including coffee cans and food cans (commonly referred to as "tin" cans). Again, the cans should be rinsed with water and flattened to conserve storage space. Approximately 65% of the energy needed to make steel can be saved by recycling steel cans.

It is best that you contact your local recyclers to find out which ones accept paper, glass, plastic, and metal items and to find out exactly how certain items may need to be separated. For instance, some recycling centers will accept mixed plastics, mixed glass and mixed metals, while others require separation in various ways. Some recyclers only function as a drop-off center for certain recyclables and will not pay for all items they receive.

Many of the homeowners who do not live in areas where the local sanitation department makes curbside collections of recyclables, purchase the types of containers which they prefer to use for separately storing their recyclables. Others simply use plastic bags, such as those in which their groceries are carried, to separately store flattened aluminum cans, glass, "tin" cans, etc. Even the plastic grocery bags can be saved and returned to most large groceries for re-use or recycling. (At least one of the supermarket chain stores in my area deducts five cents from their customers' grocery bills for every plastic grocery bag returned to the stores.) When a sufficient quantity of recyclables are accumulated, the homeowners deliver them to a recycling center. As a convenience for those who are not interested in being paid for their recyclables, a number of communities locate drop-off facilities in parking lots adjacent to supermarkets. The State of California has passed an innovative beverage container recycling law which requires new recycling facilities to be established within one-half mile of every major supermarket in the state.

On the other hand, a number of municipalities (including some in California) have initiated curbside recycling collection programs, and many of them even provide the containers for homeowners to use for depositing their recyclable products. In some locales residents are furnished with a single container into which glass, metal cans, and newspapers are deposited, while other locations provide three containers so the homeowners can deposit these recyclables separately. Some communities and a few states have passed laws which *require* homeowners to participate in their curbside collection programs while some other communities offer cash or gift incentives to households cooperating in their voluntary curbside recycling programs.

The State of New Jersey, for instance, has a *mandatory* recycling law that requires homeowners to recycle at least three materials (typically newspapers, aluminum cans, and glass containers). This mandatory program has spurred development of new glass cullet, used paper, and aluminum plants within the state. The law encourages industries to purchase new recycling equipment by allowing them to receive a 50% tax credit. Moreover, a number of the law's provisions help stimulate markets for recyclables. As an example, at least 45% of the amount of money spent for paper purchased by the state must be spent for recycled paper.

Rockford, Illinois, has a voluntary program which incorporates a weekly garbage lottery award of $1,000 to any resident whose inspected trash bags are free of newspapers and aluminum cans. In Austin, Texas, a privately sponsored "Cash for Trash" program offers a $100 prize each day to a randomly selected household with recyclable materials set out for curbside collection. Private industry and a leading newspaper provide continuing sponsorship of this program as an ongoing incentive to encourage increasing curbside recycling participation.

The City of Dallas has 32 "Igloo" collection facilities located in shopping centers. On December 10, 1990, a ten-month pilot residential recycling program to test the feasibility of citywide curbside recycling was begun in 16 neighborhoods across Dallas. Each of the approximately 14,000 households participating in the program was given an 18-gallon plastic recycling bin. Residents are asked to put plastics, clear and colored glass, aluminum and steel cans in the bottom of the bins and newpapers on top. Dallas has adopted the nationwide EPA goal of reducing by 25% the amount of wastes sent to landfills by 1992. Although many other cities have been forced to adopt citywide recycling because of a lack of landfill space, Dallas is beginning its program primarily to save resources, according to Mayor Annette Strauss. "In traditional Dallas style, we will meet environmental goals with success," she said. "It is essential that business, government and the public work together toward a more environmentally sound future."

HOUSEHOLD HAZARDOUS WASTES (HHW)
There are thousands of household cleaning and upkeep products which contain substances which can threaten the health of humans, pets, livestock, birds, fish and the environment if they are disposed of improperly. Common items such as cleaners, detergents, hair

sprays, herbicides, paints, pesticides, solvents, paints, and do-it-yourself automotive materials are just a few of these "household hazardous wastes." If the product's label says either, "Caution," "Danger," or "Warning," it is in the hazardous waste category.

The disposal of household hazardous wastes is unregulated in most states; therefore, people typically dispose of it by pouring it on top of the ground, pouring it down drains or storm sewers, burning or burying it in the backyard, or putting it in with other household wastes to be collected by the city or a waste management company. Unfortunately, many people either do not realize the adverse environmental impact of such disposal methods, or they find it too inconvenient or costly to dispose of these hazardous materials properly. The improper disposal of HHW can cause a number of problems, including corrosion of plumbing materials, toxic fumes, problems in septic systems and at wastewater treatment plants, ground and surface water pollution, fires, explosions and toxic emissions, to mention just a few.

Many municipalities have designated certain days as "HHW Collection Day." On collection days, citizens are invited to bring their household hazardous wastes to specified locations for recycling or disposal by professional waste handlers. More and more communities are establishing permanent collection sites (e.g. fire stations, landfills, county property) to collect HHW. If your community has not established either of the above collection programs, contact your local Extension Service, and it will be happy to mail you the recommended disposal methods for your state.

USED OIL

Used oil is not currently a federally listed hazardous waste, but it is a valuable resource that should be recycled for several reasons. Used oil can contain a number of materials that can cause harm to human health and the environment if disposed of improperly. For instance, pouring oil down storm drains, onto the ground, or into the trash can contaminate ground water, surface water, and soils. The EPA estimates that do-it-yourselfers who change their own oil generate 200 million gallons of used oil per year, yet only about 10% of such used oil is recycled. That means that 180 million gallons per year are poured onto the ground, down sewers, or into the trash, thus causing the above mentioned contaminations.

Recycling used oil saves energy and natural resources and reduces our dependence on foreign oil. Used oil can be re-refined into lubricating oil and used again as motor oil or reprocessed and used as fuel in industrial burners and boilers. It takes only one gallon of used oil to make the 2-1/2 quarts of lubricating oil that it takes 42 gallons of crude oil to make and only about one-third of the energy required to refine crude oil to lubricant quality. The EPA estimates that if all of the used oil in the U.S. were recycled, it would save the U.S. 1.3 million barrels of oil per day!

Many service stations and businesses that specialize in quick oil changes and some auto-parts stores will accept used oil for recycling.

The State of Alabama's Project ROSE (Recycled Oil Saves Energy) has grown from two pilot used-oil projects to national prominence. Project ROSE was designed to collect used oil from individual, corporate, and municipal consumers, garages, and service stations for treatment by a used-oil processor. It is a non-profit conservation program that was initiated by Alabama's Science, Technology and Energy Division, Department of Economic and Community Affairs, and sponsored by the University of Alabama. The project utilizes curbside collection (in some cities), collection centers, and 55-gallon drum placement on the premises of cooperating businesses and small government agencies in rural areas.

❖

There are a number of other success stories of communities' recycling achievements all across our country, with some of the communities having already reduced the volumes of wastes sent to landfills by 25% or more. Some of the programs were started by necessity due to closings of landfills, others to forestall landfill closings, and still others for environmental and economic benefits. The costs associated with the closing of landfills in two cities on the West Coast, for instance, are expected to run from about $50 million to as high as $90 million. Needless to say, these two cities have implemented aggressive recycling programs to lessen their future dependence on landfills.

Improperly operated landfills have been linked to soil, surface, and groundwater contamination, and insufficient pollution controls on incinerators has led to air quality problems. New landfill sites are becoming increasingly difficult to locate because of the public's "not in my back yard" opposition. The stricter landfill design and operation regulations proposed by the EPA are expected to close many existing facilities, as well as to increase the cost of new landfills. The Texas Department of Health, for instance, estimates that approximately one-third of the 900 landfills in Texas will have to close if the proposed revisions are adopted.

The closing of landfills, the anticipated increased number of closings, more strict operating criteria and the siting difficulties for new landfills has led to steadily increasing tipping fees (the amount charged to dispose of a ton of waste) around the country. Less than ten years ago, the national average tipping fee was about $10 per ton. Now the national average is close to $30 per ton, and in some areas the tipping fee is almost six times that amount.

Boy Scouts, Girl Scouts, the Sierra Club, the Audubon Society and many other national and local groups are actively encouraging their members to participate in recycling and to assist the general public in participating in local recycling programs. Many national industries and local businesses lend their support both financially and through their direct involvement in recycling their own waste products. However, none of these programs can be successful without the participation of the local citizens. Join with these groups, work with your local government officials and encourage others to participate in these recycling programs. Get involved in doing some kind of volunteer work. Helping those who are less fortunate, or just helping our communities in general by donating our time for needed projects is very rewarding.

I cannot imagine any human beings who do not enjoy being successful. Whether they be athletes or artists, blue-collar workers or bosses, farmers or horticulturists, heads of state or housewives, salespersons or scientists, or students or teachers, all enjoy the satisfaction realized from achieving that which they set out to do. Just by creatively working to solve a problem and by knowing we are contributing to a worthwhile effort, we can realize a satisfying sense of accomplishment. Every time we mow our lawns and leave the clippings in the lawn, or every time we use the grass clippings as a mulch or to make compost, we know we are helping to solve the landfill crisis and we feel good about ourselves. Every day that we save our newspapers for recycling, along with cans, glass, and plastic products, we know we are being successful in prolonging the life of our landfills and that we are helping to improve our environment and the wellbeing of future generations.

Every country on earth, including our country, has a multitude of disturbing problems which must be addressed and solved. Acid rain, AIDS, air pollution, bank failures, bigotry, child abuse, crime, destruction of forests, drinking water contamination, drugs, DWI, homeless people, illiteracy, inflation, recession, soil contamination, and waste disposal are but a few. None of these problems are impossible to solve. All we need to do is get enough people concerned and *involved* in *doing* something, individually and collectively, working with our law enforcement and other governmental agencies and with other concerned individuals and groups. Granted, some of these problems are not easy to fix, and it will take time to fix them.

However, we *can* fix the waste disposal problem almost immediately by recycling our yard wastes and kitchen wastes in our own back yards, and by participating in the recycling of the other household wastes such as, glass, metal, paper and plastic products, and our used oil. We can do it. We *will* do it because *we care* and because we are *Americans.* God blessed us with a land of plenty. Let's keep it that way.

❖

APPENDIX 1

NATIONWIDE LISTING OF COOPERATIVE EXTENSION SERVICE LOCATIONS

If you do not know how to contact your nearest Agricultural Extension Service's office, you can contact your state's Cooperative Extension Service listed below.

ALABAMA
Auburn University
Duncan Hall
Auburn, AL 36849
205-826-4444

ALASKA
University of Alaska
Fairbanks, AK 99775
907-474-7246

ARIZONA
University of Arizona
College of Agriculture
Forbes Bldg.
Tucson, AZ 85721
602-621-7205

ARKANSAS
University of Arkansas
1201 McAlmont, PO Box 391
Little Rock, AR 72203
501-373-2500

CALIFORNIA
300 Lakeside Dr. – 6th Floor
Oakland, CA 94612
415-987-0060

COLORADO
Colorado State University
Fort Collins, CO 80523
303-491-6281

CONNECTICUT
University of Connecticut
1376 Storrs Rd.
W B Young Bldg, Box U-36
Storrs, CT 06268
203-486-4125

DELAWARE
University of Delaware
Townsend Hall
Newark, DE 19717
302-451-2504

DISTRICT OF COLUMBIA
University of the District of Columbia
901 Newton St. NE
Washington, DC 20017
202-576-6993

FLORIDA
University of Florida
Institute of Food & Ag Sciences
McCarty Hall
Gainesville, FL 32611
904-392-1761

GEORGIA
University of Georgia
College of Agriculture
Athens, GA 30602
404-542-3824

HAWAII
University of Hawaii at Manoa
Honolulu, HI 96822
808-948-8397

IDAHO
University of Idaho
Ag Science Bldg
Moscow, ID 83843
208-885-6639

ILLINOIS
University of Illinois
1301 W Gregory
Mumford Hall
Urbana, IL 61801
217-333-2660

INDIANA
Purdue University
West Lafayette, IN 47906
317-494-8488

IOWA
Iowa State University
110 Curtiss
Ames, IA 50011
515-294-4576

ersity

، 66506

KY
.ty of Kentucky
e of Agriculture
.gton, KY 40546
-257-9000

LOUISIANA
Louisiana State University
Knapp Hall
University Station
Baton Rouge, LA 70803
504-388-6083

MAINE
University of Maine
Winslow Hall
Orono, ME 04469
207-581-3191

MARYLAND
University of Maryland
College Park, MD 20742
301-454-3742

MASSACHUSETTS
College of Food & Natural Resources
University of Massachusetts
Amherst, MA 01003
413-545-4800

MICHIGAN
Michigan State University
Agriculture Hall
East Lansing, MI 48824
517-355-2308

MINNESOTA
University of Minnesota
Coffey Hall
St. Paul, MN 55108
612-373-1223

MISSISSIPPI
Mississippi State University
PO Box 5446
Mississippi State, MS 39762
601-325-3036

MISSOURI
University of Missouri
University Hall
Columbia, MO 65211
314-882-7754

MONTANA
Montana State University
College of Agriculture
Bozeman, MT 59717
406-994-3681

NEBRASKA
University of Nebraska
Agricultural Hall
Lincoln, NE 68583
402-472-2966

NEVADA
College of Agriculture
University of Nevada-Reno
Reno, NV 89557
702-784-6611

NEW HAMPSHIRE
University of New Hampshire
College of Life Sciences & Agriculture
Durham, NH 03824
603-862-1520

NEW JERSEY
Rutgers University
Cook College
PO Box 231
New Brunswick, NJ 08903
201-932-9306

NEW MEXICO
New Mexico State University
Box 3AE
Las Cruces, NM 88003
505-646-1806

NEW YORK
Cornell University
Roberts Hall
Ithaca, NY 14853
607-255-2117

NORTH CAROLINA
North Carolina State University
Box 7602, Ricks Hall
Raleigh, NC 27695
919-737-2811

NORTH DAKOTA
North Dakota State University
Box 5437
Fargo, ND 58105
701-237-8944

OHIO
Ohio State University
2120 Fyffe Rd.
Columbus, OH 43210
614-292-4067

OKLAHOMA
Oklahoma State University
Agricultural Hall
Stillwater, OK 74078
405-624-5400

OREGON
Oregon State University
Ballard Hall
Corvallis, OR 97331
503-754-2711

PENNSYLVANIA
Pennsylvania State University
323 Ag Administration Building
University Park, PA 16802
814-863-3438

PUERTO RICO
University of Puerto Rico
College of Agricultural Sciences
Mayaguez, PR 00708
809-832-4040

RHODE ISLAND
University of Rhode Island
Woodward Hall
Kingston, RI 02881
401-792-2815

SOUTH CAROLINA
Clemson University
Barre Hall
Clemson, SC 29634
803-656-3382

SOUTH DAKOTA
Box 2207
Brookings, SD 57007
605-688-4792

TENNESSEE
University of Tennessee
PO Box 1071
Morgan Hall
Knoxville, Tn 37901
615-974-7114

TEXAS
Texas A&M University
College Station, TX 77843
409-845-7808

UTAH
Utah State University
Logan, UT 84322
801-750-2200

VERMONT
University of Vermont
College of Agriculture
178 S. Prospect St.
Burlington, VT 05401
802-656-3036

VIRGINIA
Virginia Polytechnic Institute and
   State University
Burruss Hall
Blacksburg, VA 24061
703-961-6705

WASHINGTON
College of Agriculture
Washington State University
Pullman, WA 99164
509-335-2811

WEST VIRGINIA
West Virginia University
Morgantown, WV 26506
304-293-5691

WISCONSIN
University of Wisconsin
432 N Lake St.
Madison, WI 53706
608-263-2775

WYOMING
University of Wyoming
Box 3354, University Station
Laramie, WY 82071
307-766-5124

APPENDIX 2

NATIONWIDE LISTING OF
STATE RECYCLING OFFICES

ALABAMA
Department of Environmental Management
Solid Waste Division
1715 Congressman Wm.
Dickinson Drive
Montgomery, AL 36130
205-271-7700

ALASKA
Department of Environmental Conservation
Solid Waste Program
P.O. Box O
Juneau, AK 99811-1800
907-465-2671

ARIZONA
Department of Environmental Quality –
  O.W.P.
Waste Planning Section, 4th Floor
Phoenix, AZ 85004
602-257-2317

ARKANSAS
Department of Pollution Control and
  Ecology
Solid Waste Division
8001 National Drive
Little Rock, AR 72219
501-562-7444

CALIFORNIA
Recycling Division
Department of Conservation
819 19th Street
Sacramento, CA 95814
916-323-3743

COLORADO
Department of Health
4210 E. 11th Avenue
Denver, CO 80220
303-320-4830

CONNECTICUT
Recycling Program
Department of Environmental Protection
Hartford, CT 06106
203-566-8722

DELAWARE
Department of Natural Resources and
  Environmental Control
89 Kings Highway
P.O. Box 1401
Dover, DE 19903
302-736-4794

DISTRICT OF COLUMBIA
Public Space and Maintenance
  Administration
4701 Shepard Parkway, S.W.
Washington, DC 20032
202-767-8512

FLORIDA
Department of Environmental Regulation
2600 Blairstone Road
Tallahassee, FL 32201
904-488-0300

GEORGIA
Department of Community Affairs
40 Marietta St. N.W., 8th Floor
Atlanta, GA 30303
404-656-3898

HAWAII
Litter Control Office
Department of Health
205 Koula Street
Honolulu, HI 96813
808-548-3400

IDAHO
Department of Environmental Quality
Hazardous Materials Bureau
450 W. State Street
Boise, ID 83720
208-334-5879

ILLINOIS
Illinois EPA
Land Pollution Control Division
2200 Churchill Road
P.O. Box 19276
Springfield, IL 62706
217-782-6761

INDIANA
Office of Solid and Hazardous Waste
    Management
Department of Environmental Management
105 S. Meridian Street
Indianapolis, IN 46225
317-232-8883

IOWA
Department of Natural Resources
Waste Management Division
Wallace State Office Building
Des Moines, IA 50319
515-281-8176

KANSAS
Bureau of Waste Management
Department of Health and Environment
Topeka, KS 66620
913-296-1594

KENTUCKY
Resources Management Branch
Division of Waste Management
18 Reilly Road
Frankfort, KY 40601
502-564-6716

LOUISIANA
Department of Environmental Quality
P.O. Box 44307
Baton Rouge, LA 70804
504-342-1216

MAINE
Office of Waste Reduction and Recycling
Department of Economic and Community
    Development
State House Station #130
Augusta, ME 04333
207-289-2111

MARYLAND
Department of Environment
Hazardous and Solid Waste Administration
2500 Broening Highway – Building 40
Baltimore, MD 21224
301-631-3343

MASSACHUSETTS
Division of Solid Waste Management
    D.E.Q.E.
1 Winter Street, 4th Floor
Boston, MA 02108
617-292-5962

MICHIGAN
Waste Management Division
Department of Natural Resources
P.O. Box 30028
Lansing, MI 48909
517-373-0540

MINNESOTA
Pollution Control Agency
520 Lafayette Road
St. Paul, MN 55155
612-296-6300

MISSISSIPPI
Non-Hazardous Waste Section
Bureau of Pollution Control
Department of Natural Resources
P.O. Box 10385
Jackson, MS 39209
601-961-5047

MISSOURI
Department of Natural Resources
P.O. Box 176
Jefferson City, MO 65102
314-751-3176

MONTANA
Solid Waste Program
Department of Health and Environmental
    Science
Cogswell Building, Room B201
Helena, MT 59620
406-444-2821

NEBRASKA
Litter Reduction and Recycling Programs
Department of Environmental Control
P.O. Box 98922
Lincoln, NE 68509
402-471-4210

NEVADA
Energy Extension Service
Office of Community Service
1100 S. Williams Street
Carson City, NV 89710
702-885-4420

NEW HAMPSHIRE
Waste Management Division
Department of Environmental Services
6 Hazen Drive
Concord, NH 03301
603-271-2900

NEW JERSEY
Office of Recycling
Department of Environmental Protection
CN 414
401 E. State Street
Trenton, NJ 08625
609-292-0331

NEW MEXICO
Solid Waste Section
Environmental Improvement Division
1190 St. Francis Drive
Sante Fe, NM 87503
505-457-2780

NEW YORK
Bureau of Waste Reduction and Recycling
Department of Environmental Conservation
50 Wolf Road, Room 208
Albany, NY 12233
518-457-7337

NORTH CAROLINA
Solid Waste Management Branch
Department of Human Resources
P.O. Box 2091
Raleigh, NC 27602
919-733-0692

NORTH DAKOTA
Division of Waste Management
Department of Health
1200 Missouri Avenue, Room 302
Box 5520
Bismark, ND 58502-5520
701-224-2366

OHIO
Division of Litter Prevention and Recycling
Ohio EPA
Fountain Square Building, E-1
Columbus, OH 43224
614-265-7061

OKLAHOMA
Solid Waste Division
Department of Health
1000 N.E. 10th Street
Oklahoma City, OK 73152
405-271-7159

OREGON
Department of Environmental Quality
811 S.W. Sixth
Portland, OR 97204
503-229-5913

PENNSYLVANIA
Waste Reduction and Recycling Section
Division of Waste Minimization and
    Planning
Department of Environmental Resources
P.O. Box 2063
Harrisburg, PA 17120
717-787-7382

RHODE ISLAND
Office of Environmental Coordination
Department of Environmental Management
83 Park Street
Providence, RI 02903
401-277-3434

SOUTH CAROLINA
Department of Health and Environmental
    Control
2600 Bull Street
Columbia, SC 29201
803-734-5200

SOUTH DAKOTA
Energy Office
217-1/2 West Missouri
Pierre, SD 57501
605-773-3603

TENNESSEE
Department of Public Health
Division of Solid Waste Management
Customs House, 4th Floor
701 Broadway
Nashville, TN 37219-5403
615-741-3424

TEXAS
Division of Solid Waste Management
Department of Health
1100 W. 49th Street
Austin, TX 78756
512-458-7271

UTAH
Bureau of Solid and Hazardous Waste
Department of Environmental Health
P.O. Box 16690
Salt Lake City, UT 84116-0690
801-538-6170

VERMONT
Agency of National Recources
103 S. Main Street, West Building
Waterbury, VT 05676
802-244-8702

VIRGINIA
Department of Waste Management
Division of Litter Control and Recycling
11th Floor, Monroe Building
101 N. 14th Street
Richmond, VA 23219
1-800-Keepit

WASHINGTON
Department of Ecology
Mail Stop PV-11
Olympia, WA 95804
1-800-Recycle

WEST VIRGINIA
Department of Natural Resources
Conservation, Education, and Litter
    Control
1800 Washington Street E.
Charleston, WV 25305
304-348-3370

WISCONSIN
Department of Natural Resources
P.O. Box 7921
Madison, WI 53707
608-266-5741

WYOMING
Solid Waste Management Program
Department of Environmental Quality
Herschler Building
122 W. 25th Street
Cheyenne, WY 82002
307-777-7752

——————— ❖ ———————

REFERENCES AND RECOMMENDED READINGS

Cotner, Samuel D., Ph.D., *Container Vegetables.* Waco, Texas: TG Press, 1987.

Cotner, Samuel D., Ph.D., *The Vegetable Book.* Waco, Texas: TG Press, 1985.

Golueke, Clarence G., Ph.D., *Composting—A Study of the Process and Its Principles.* Emmaus, Pennsylvania: Rodale Press, Inc., 1972.

Knoop, William E., Ph.D., *The Complete Guide To Texas Lawn Care.* Waco, Texas: TG Press, 1986.

McGraw-Hill Encyclopedia of Science and Technology, Vol. 8 and Vol. 16. New York, New York: McGraw-Hill Book Company, 1987.

Poincelot, Raymond P., *Horticulture Principles and Practical Applications.* Englewood Cliffs, New Jersey: Prentice-Hall, Inc. 1980.

Poindexter, J.S., *Microbiology—An Introduction to Protists.* New York, New York: The Macmillan Company, 1971.

Rodale, J.I. & Staff, *The Complete Book of Composting.* Emmaus, Pennsylvania: Rodale Books, Inc., 1960.

Rodale, J.I. & Staff, *Encyclopedia of Organic Gardening.* Emmaus, Pennsylvania: Rodale Books, Inc., 1978.

Sagan, Dorion and Margulis, Lynn, *Garden of Microbial Delights.* Orlando, Florida: Harcourt Brace Jovanovich, Inc., 1988.

Sperry, Neil, *Neil Sperry's Complete Guide To Texas Gardening.* Dallas, Texas: Taylor Publishing Company, 1991.

Various publications of the Texas Agricultural Extension Service were researched for authoritative purposes, as were various Environmental Protection Agency documents. The EPA documents of particular significance were *Yard Waste Composting—A Study of Eight Programs,* which was prepared by Alison C. Taylor and Richard M. Kashmanian, Ph.D.; *This Compost Went to Market,* which was prepared by Richard M. Kashmanian, Ph.D., H. Clark Gregory, Ph.D., and Steven A. Dressing; *Decision-Makers Guide to Solid Waste Management,* which was prepared by ICF Incorporated in cooperation with the EPA's Office of Solid Waste; and *Recycling Works!— State and Local Solutions to Solid Waste Management Problems,* which was prepared by the Office of Solid Waste with the assistance of the states' recycling program managers.

Index

❖

Sunnyvale Press
P.O. Box 851971
Mesquite, Texas 75185–1971

Please send me ___ copies of *Don't Waste Your Wastes — Compost 'em* at $10.95 per copy, plus $2.00 for shipping and handling. *Please print.*

Name _____

Street _____

City _____ State _____ Zip _____

Sunnyvale Press
P.O. Box 851971
Mesquite, Texas 75185–1971

Please send me ___ copies of *Don't Waste Your Wastes — Compost 'em* at $10.95 per copy, plus $2.00 for shipping and handling. *Please print.*

Name _____

Street _____

City _____ State _____ Zip _____

Sunnyvale Press
P.O. Box 851971
Mesquite, Texas 75185–1971

Please send me ___ copies of *Don't Waste Your Wastes — Compost 'em* at $10.95 per copy, plus $2.00 for shipping and handling. *Please print.*

Name _____

Street _____

City _____ State _____ Zip _____